SIMPLY ESSENTIAL FUNERAL PLANNING KIT

DATE DUE

Don S. Cochrane

Self-Counsel Press
(a division of)
International Self-Counsel Press Ltd.
USA   Canada

Self-Counsel Press acknowledges the financial support of the Government of Canada through the Book Publishing Industry Development Program (BPIDP) for our publishing activities.

Printed in Canada.

First edition: 2002

Canadian Cataloguing in Publication Data

Cochrane, Don S. (Don Stevenson), 1933-
    Simply essential funeral planning kit

    (Self-counsel series)
    ISBN 1-55180-382-8

    1. Funeral rites and ceremonies — Planning. I. Title. II. Series.
    GT3213.A2C63   2002   393'.9   C2002-910724-5

Cremation Statistics and maps from the Cremation Association of North America are used by permission.

Every effort has been made to obtain permission for quoted material and illustrations. If there is an omission or error, the author and publisher would be grateful to be so informed.

Self-Counsel Press
(a division of)
International Self-Counsel Press Ltd.

1704 N. State Street
Bellingham, WA 98225
USA

1481 Charlotte Road
North Vancouver, BC V7J 1H1
Canada

CONTENTS

INTRODUCTION

Providing funeral services may not be considered the world's oldest profession, but it must rank among the first. Since the dawn of civilization, every known culture and religion has been faced with the problem of disposing of human remains and coping with the emotional impact of death.

The funeral rites, ceremonies, and beliefs surrounding the subject of death are a strong part of our basic culture and beliefs. Death and life both ask the question, "where did we come from and where do we go?" Death, therefore, has two dimensions: physical and spiritual. Over the past century in North America, we follow similar practices and procedures of burial and religiously oriented ceremonies of our ancestors. In the first part of the century, we focused on grief and loss with an emphasis on the afterlife. In the past 50 years, there have been major changes in the public's views and expectations surrounding funerals.

This book is part of the *Simply Essential* series. Death is the last essential act of life. My task is to help you deal with the physical and emotional problems associated with death. This book will help you, not only to talk about death, but will encourage you to discuss it with others (family, lawyer, or executor). It will allow you to express your wishes for your funeral when death comes, as inevitably it must. You will close the final chapter of your life knowing your needs and expectations for dignity will be met, and will celebrate your life in a manner and at a cost befitting your beliefs and lifestyle.

This book has three goals:

1. To help you understand that a funeral is a purchase; in fact, it is a number of purchases in two distinct areas:

   a) *Services* that include consultation concerning legal requirements (certificates, registrations, and any other necessary documentation) and the transportation of the body from the place of death to a suitable location pending the completion of funeral arrangements.

   b) *Goods* that include the purchase of items such as a casket, cemetery plot, cremation urn, or burial vault.

2. To provide full, unbiased, and up-to-date information on all options available in the areas of goods and services.

3. To help and encourage you to establish a written plan designed to deal with all aspects of your funeral arrangements, including cost, so that you may include that plan with your legal will and share it with your executor or loved ones.

This guide will provide you with the necessary information to ensure that your wishes in all three areas are carried out with the greatest degree of dignity and of consolation to your loved ones, and will provide you with an understanding of the costs involved.

Estimates suggest that 40 percent of people between the ages of 40 and 59 do not have a will. I suspect that an even smaller number has discussed or investigated a funeral plan. Estate, financial, and retirement planners all advise people to draw up a will as part of those strategies. (For more information on drawing up a will, see the *Wills Guide for Canada* or the *Complete Canadian Wills Kit*, both published by Self-Counsel Press.) It is my belief, based on my experience as a funeral director and a family counselor, that the completion of a funeral plan is a necessary step in that full process.

The funeral process can be broken into three steps:

1. The immediate disposition of the body

2. Conducting of services or ceremonies of remembrance

3. The final disposition by either cremation or burial

A funeral involves the purchase of specialized goods and services at a time of high emotional vulnerability. For that reason, a pre-need plan is the best way to ensure that your funeral will meet your expectations with full consideration of your beliefs and preferences and also take into account cost and legal requirements. That plan can be elaborate or simple, traditional, or modern, high or low cost, but it will have one essential goal: peace of mind that your last act will be one that you have personally written and meets your approval.

The first two chapters discuss the reasons to plan your funeral and test your current knowledge using a short questionnaire. Subsequent chapters deal with the public's traditional attitude toward funeral procedures and how those attitudes have changed dramatically in the past 50 years. The funeral service industry itself has changed to meet these new attitudes and values. These factors may challenge your existing assumptions about arrangements for your own funeral or that of a loved one.

This guide also contains information about the modern funeral industry. You will learn that a funeral can be stark or lavish, and that you have a wide range of options between those two choices. One of the greatest problems in dealing with funeral planning is the complication caused by having too many choices. Like a menu, the more options available, the more difficult the choice. This book attempts to simplify and clarify those choices. By following the step-by-step process provided, you can choose within each of the three main areas that form the basis of your personal funeral plan.

Chapter 5 clearly defines the duties and the expectations to be placed on either your legally appointed executor or on family or friends that have been designated to be in charge of your funeral arrangements.

Chapter 6 explains the various services and merchandise involved in the today's funeral industry and allows you to create your own package based on the wide range of available options. A full chapter discusses, in detail, the cost of each of the goods and services offered. You will learn the difference between choosing an existing package and creating an individual package, and the total cost of each. I share my experience in my local community to teach you the steps necessary to ensure that, by comparison shopping, you have a clear picture of all costs before making a final decision.

Some commonly asked questions are answered in Chapter 8, and appendixes include checklists and sample forms for various necessary functions in the process to help you organize information and create a full plan that includes financial costs. A glossary provides terms and words that may be unfamiliar and, finally, a list of Web sites and books that provide additional information is included.

More than one person at the same time can use this book. A married couple or different family members might decide on entirely different plans. One spouse may wish a traditional religious service conducted by a full-service funeral home. This might include embalming, public viewing, a specific choice of casket, and burial in a cemetery. The other spouse might opt for simplicity with cremation, a gathering of friends or no gathering at all, and the burial or scattering of the remains. Either plan is valid and represents the beliefs and wishes of the individual. Both options can be arranged together so that, regardless which spouse dies first, the individual and personalized plan of each will be used.

After you read the book, you will be ready to write your funeral plan by completing two of the three funeral statements. These simple and direct statements clearly indicate your choices and preferences concerning each phase and detail of the funeral process. It indicates the costs that you consider appropriate and names the funeral service provider that you have chosen to entrust with your plan.

I hope that by using this resource book, you will be more knowledgeable and therefore better prepared to deal with this inevitable and important life event and to make your family and/or executor aware that you have dealt with this matter.

A written funeral plan, added to a current will and a clear indication of your financial assets and liabilities will ensure that your family is in the best possible situation to deal with your death. You will have planned ahead to deal with life's final transaction.

1
WHY PLAN YOUR FUNERAL?

Every day we are faced with problems to solve, an endless variety of things to learn, and a list of seemingly endless tasks. Some tasks are necessary and we must deal with ourselves, and some we can delegate, but the way we deal with them indicates our attitudes and life skills. One of the most important life skills is the ability to plan. Lord Baden Powell, the founder of the Boy Scout movement, chose "be prepared" as a motto. Preparation can mean the difference between success and failure.

I have been a counselor for over 40 years in education, addiction, job displacement, and family practice. I began counseling, however, as a funeral director, and with my half-century of training and experience, I have found that there are several simple steps in effective problem-solving regardless of the situation, the degree of crisis, or the size of the problem. Those steps are as follows:

- Understand the reality of the situation and the problem that is facing you. Knowledge is the key to understanding so learn all you can about your options. If you are concerned that your emotions are clouding your view of the situation, look for help to separate reality from misconception.

- Investigate and list the resources that are available to you in finding a solution.

- Create a plan and write it down. Set a direction and an objective: the plan should be a clear statement of what you want to do and how you want to do it. Be flexible. You can always adjust the plan if circumstances change.

The six keys to funeral planning:

1. Overcome your reluctance

2. Plan ahead

3. Comparison shop

4. Know your rights

5. Resist unwanted pressure

6. Avoid emotional spending

- Communicate your plan and its objectives to the people who will be impacted by your plan.

This simple sequence of actions is effective whether you wish to change a behavior, settle a dispute, or complete a business transaction. Regardless of circumstances, if you follow this process of problem solving, the outcome will always be better than a knee-jerk reaction or avoiding the problem.

This book approaches funeral planning in exactly the same way. It outlines the problems created by your death. Unpleasant as the thought may be, death is a reality and a certainty. This guide will encourage you to understand the potential problems encountered by those left with the task of dealing with your death. It defines the available resources and options and the cost of each. It will help you to write a clear plan, outline your preferences and choices, and deal with the physical, emotional, and financial impacts of your death or the death of a loved one. Finally, it will encourage you to communicate that plan to those left in charge of your affairs.

Ten Reasons to Plan Your Funeral

Using this simple process outlined above to create a plan while you are still alive, you can accomplish ten important goals that will bring you peace of mind that you have completed your life on your terms.

1. No one is in a better position than you are, while you are alive, to gather the information, documents, and background material that will be needed when you die.

2. It is the only way to see that your preferences and values in life are reflected in the final event for which you will be remembered.

3. It removes the risk that members of your family might have different views on this event. It is an affirmative statement by you that, coupled with your legal will, ensures that your wishes will be respected by the law and by those you love.

4. It ensures that the emotional impact of your death will not cloud the financial considerations involved in the purchase of goods and services at the time of your death.

5. It leaves a clear message concerning the manner, degree, and type of commemorative service that you desire: religious, secular, or no service at all.

6. It allows you to choose the people involved in your funeral. This could include the person with the prime responsibility for carrying out your wishes — your executor or another person you so designate — any one else you might want to participate as a master of ceremonies or pallbearer.

7. It clearly defines your choices in the major areas of arrangement:
   - Burial or cremation: plot, buried or scattered ashes, urn, monument, etc.
   - Direct disposition or religious or secular services prior to disposition
   - Casket or burial or cremation container
   - Open or closed casket
8. It outlines your views on the memorial service on such matters as —
   - floral tributes,
   - donations to charities in lieu of flowers, and
   - music.
9. It allows you to shop for the goods and services, before they are required. You can make cost comparisons on all aspects of the funeral and show the financial implications of one choice versus another.
10. It gives you the satisfaction of knowing that "you did it your way" and didn't leave the arrangements for others.

Preplanning your funeral is the business of conducting your affairs so that your loved ones have less to deal with after your death. It is cost-efficient and can be conducted in a relaxed atmosphere so you have the time to consider all options. I believe it is simply essential to the well-being of those you love.

We all have common needs in the midst of a crisis but we may have very different ways to cope with them.

Overcoming Your Fear of Dealing with Death

In Chapter 2, you will complete a questionnaire that will help you understand the number of choices and decisions that the person responsible for your funeral must face. That person could be a spouse, a child, a friend, or several family members. Without a funeral plan, that person is working under a number of handicaps.

He or she will be dealing with the emotional impact of your death, whether it has been the result of a long illness or is sudden and unexpected. He or she will be experiencing the emotional impact of grief. Everyone experiences different degrees of grief but all feel shock and disbelief. Some may cry, or feel pain or physical distress. Some may experience anger or may be preoccupied and not wish to deal with details and choices. Some may even experience feelings of guilt and depression and may want to withdraw and rest. While in this state, the person responsible for your funeral will be asked to make many decisions.

You should be the one to make those decisions and choices before your death and in a calm atmosphere. Armed with knowledge and advice prior to the event, you can make rational and financially sound decisions tailored to your personal beliefs. By purchasing this book, you have

Review and, if necessary, adjust both your will and your funeral plan every few years.

taken the first step in completing a funeral plan that will meet your needs and wishes and remove that heavy burden from your loved ones. Ideally, you will have already completed two of the three steps concerning death: the first is the completion of a legal will; the second is the purchase of life insurance. Your funeral plan is the third step that completes that process.

You may be saying, "That makes sense, but I am still having a hard time with this. I am willing to get information but can't move on to the next step. I am willing to discuss it, but to actually go to a funeral home or meet with a representative from a memorial society, is asking a lot." You might add, "My spouse or the other family members are even less keen than I am."

The subject of death raises fears for many people. That is a natural reaction. If you are unafraid of dealing with this issue and even anxious to get prepared, then there is no problem. If, however, you need to discuss your plans with loved ones, then you should understand their reluctance or even refusal. By going ahead yourself, you will ease the completion of your plan and later gain their support for your efforts.

There are three emotional obstacles in planning a funeral: denial, procrastination, and avoidance.

Denial

Elisabeth Kubler-Ross, in her best-selling book, *On Death and Dying*, describes the stages of grief. The first stage is denial. We build defense systems against things that threaten or frighten us. Our greatest fear is our own death or the deaths of those we love. One of the defenses we use against this fear is denial. Like the child that says, "If I close my eyes, you can't see me," denial is our way of closing our eyes to reality. To deal with any problem, we must see it, understand it, and then create solutions to deal with it. All of those coping steps are blocked if we deny the existence of the problem.

Friends and family may claim that the event is a long way off and they will deal with it when it happens. They are denying the inevitability of death. No one knows when death will occur. It could be a long time from now or it could happen soon.

There are a number of emotions that we experience when dealing with death but denial is one of the most powerful and must be overcome. Death is the ultimate and final reality. Acceptance of that reality is the key to moving on.

Procrastination

Another emotional defense in dealing with death is procrastination. To some people, "putting it off" is a way of life. After all, there is always tomorrow. The problem with this defense is that it is simply not valid.

Death is one of those life experiences that cannot be put off to another day. Your loved ones will be forced to deal with your death immediately while they themselves are in a critical state. For you, tomorrow will have ceased to exist, but arrangements must be made quickly for the disposition of your body. Some situations cannot be put off.

A well-known saying states that the only two certainties in life are death and taxes. That isn't quite true, because a good accountant may help delay or even avoid taxes, but no one can avoid death and the immediate consequences that arise from it. Your funeral director can, however, help you to deal with it.

Avoidance

The third defense is avoidance, which creates several problems. The first is that because you wouldn't discuss your funeral while you were alive, someone else will have to deal with it when you are dead. Your avoidance means that no important decisions were made concerning your choices of burial or cremation, memorial service, and the final disposition of your remains. Another problem arises when different family members have different views on what you might have wanted. This can lead to family tensions and divisions at a time when loved ones should be drawing close.

It is amazing that so many married couples delay talking about and acting upon the eventuality of death. Refusing to discuss this eventuality robs the couple of the opportunity to learn the wishes and desires of the other partner. One partner might justly say to the other, "We have made every major decision together all through our married life. Why not make plans for our funerals together?"

Prearranging your funeral is your gift to your family. It is a gift of love and consideration for them at a time when they will be experiencing the impact of your loss. This gift will help them through that difficult emotional period and give them the peace of mind that you were laid to rest as you would have wished.

Sharing Your Plan with Others

When you create a funeral plan, the question may arise as to whether or not to share this exercise with others.

There are a number of options to consider:

- *Alone:* You can carry out the exercises in the book by yourself and wait until you have all the information you need to make your own choices. You can choose to discuss the plan with others during preparation to get their input or wait until the plan is complete before discussing it.

- *Couples or Partners:* You can use the information gained to create identical or different plans for each partner. This is usual with married couples.

- *Group:* The book can also be used by a discussion group to gather information, discuss the various options, and allow various points of view to be considered.

All of these approaches are equally acceptable, but for each the goal should be to share your completed plan with your legal advisor, executor, or the person responsible for your funeral arrangements. They cannot act in your best interests if they don't know that such a plan exists. Your funeral plan is not a legal document but rather a written statement of guidelines. As such, it is not binding unless it is specifically mentioned in and forms part of your legal will. Either way, your directions to those now in charge of your affairs will carry a great deal of weight should members of your family wish to choose goods and services that are not in step with your beliefs, values, and final wishes.

2
WHAT DO I KNOW?
WHAT DO I NEED TO
KNOW?

Before you create your plan, it is important to get some sense of your present views and level of knowledge. Most people's perception of the funeral industry and their choices and options are formed by their previous experiences with death. Many people assume that they should simply follow the family tradition or the way they have seen it done in the past. Others have little or no idea of what is involved as they have never arranged a funeral. The questionnaire in this chapter, "Funeral Knowledge Questionnaire," will allow you to examine the issues we will be dealing with and your current views on the subject. There are no right or wrong answers. This is not a test.

The first question that anyone wishing to explain a process, sell a product, or inform you on any subject asks is what is your level of knowledge on that subject. A real estate lawyer will ask if this is your first home purchase. A doctor may inquire if you know what high blood pressure is and what it means to you, and a decorator may ask if you have any preset ideas of what you would like. These questions define a starting point. If you have been involved in a funeral arrangement recently or know exactly what you want and what it will cost, you do not need detailed explanations.

However, your answers can give a clear indication of your level of knowledge. "This is our third house purchase and we know the process," "I think I know what high blood pressure is but I don't know what causes it or what it will do to me," and "I want everything in earth tones with no bright colors or strong contrasts" are answers that provide your advisor with your level of knowledge, and the subsequent explanations of goods or services can be more or less detailed as necessary.

This book is primarily designed for those who know little or nothing about planning a funeral as well as those who may have been involved in the past but are not aware of the many changes in the industry. Those of you who have little or no knowledge of the funeral process will be interested in all the chapters and the various components in each. Those of you who have a general idea of what you want but are open to change in such areas as burial versus cremation or the commemorative service versus no service, this will confirm your beliefs or give you an opportunity to approach them again with current data. Finally, if you know exactly what you want and are curious about the various prices and packages available, then this guide will simplify the creation of your funeral statement.

Use the "Funeral Knowledge Questionnaire" to help you assess your knowledge about funeral planning.

Funeral Knowledge Questionnaire

1. **If you died today would your next of kin or executor know whom to contact to deal with your remains and the funeral arrangements?**

   Yes ❏   No ❏   Unsure ❏

2. **Would they have the basic information to complete the forms for the registration of death (vital statistics information), obituaries, and all other information needed to plan your funeral?**

   Statistics: Yes ❏   No ❏   Unsure ❏
   Obituaries: Yes ❏   No ❏   Unsure ❏
   Arrangements: Yes ❏   No ❏   Unsure ❏

3. **Do you have the following list of documents available so that the executor or your next of kin would be able to find them and use them?**

   Current legal will: Yes ❏   No ❏   Unsure ❏

   Birth, marriage, or divorce certificates, and reliable information on significant dates:

   Yes ❏   No ❏   Unsure ❏

   Social security number, veteran's papers, etc.:

   Yes ❏   No ❏

4. **Have you chosen between burial and cremation?**

Burial ❏   Cremation ❏   Undecided ❏

5. **Do you know what type of funeral service you would prefer?**

No service ❏   Religious ❏   Family only ❏

Celebration of life ❏   Unsure ❏

6. **Do you wish to be embalmed and viewed after death?**

No ❏

or

Yes ❏   Family viewing only ❏   Public viewing ❏

7. **Do you have any knowledge of the cost ranges in your locality for the following goods or services?**

Funeral service fee: Yes ❏   No ❏   Unsure ❏

Casket or burial/cremation container:

Yes ❏   No ❏   Unsure ❏

Cemetery costs (plot, opening, closing charges, concrete or other vault):

Yes ❏   No ❏   Unsure ❏

Cremation charges (urn, memorial marker):

Yes ❏   No ❏   Unsure ❏

Other costs (taxes, death certificates, clergy fees, flowers, and obituaries)

Yes ❏   No ❏   Unsure ❏

What cost do you have in mind for your full funeral?

$ _____

8. **If you wish to be buried, do you know where? Do you own a plot and have the ownership papers?**

Yes ❏   No ❏

9. **If you wish to be cremated, do you know what you want done with your ashes? (Scattered or buried? Where, and if scattered, by whom?)**

Yes ❏   No ❏   Unsure ❏

10. **Did you know you could prepay your funeral plan, locking in the cost?**

Yes ❑   No ❑   Unsure ❑

11. **Have you ever discussed any of these topics with anyone in your family?**

Yes ❑   No ❑   Unsure ❑

If you answered "No" or "Unsure" to most of these questions, this book and a few basic inquiries within your community will quickly provide answers to complete your personal funeral plan. If you answered "Yes" to many or most of the questions, this book will help you organize your preferences and choices so that you may act upon them.

3
OPTIONS AND CHOICES

When I entered the funeral profession more than 50 years ago, the choices available to the person arranging a funeral were very limited. The word "traditional" describes the process that was followed. The choice of funeral home was usually based on previous family contact. It might even be based on religion, ethnic preferences, or a personal friendship with the owner or an employee.

Once that initial choice was made, the purchaser could expect to follow a path set by custom and consistency. The body would be embalmed, clothed, and placed in a casket for public or private viewing. The funeral service was usually conducted by a cleric along well-established ritual guidelines.

Burial was the overwhelming choice for final disposal and separate arrangements were made with the cemetery, as was the purchase of a monument.

In the sixties and seventies, changes began to occur in a number of areas but, most important, the public perception of death, dying, and the funeral service industry underwent a transformation. The religious convictions and beliefs of a great deal of the North American population were altered. A funeral ceased to be a ritual focused on an afterlife and became instead one that celebrated the accomplishments of this life.

The industry itself found that several fads from outside the business grew into trends that continue to expand. A number of those trends are in the areas of cremation, planning, and memorial or commemorative

Except in certain cases, embalming is not a legal requirement.

service styles. Today there are more closed caskets, donations to charities in lieu of flowers, and a growing number of prearranged funerals. Funeral services have changed due to religious and multicultural practices as well as nonreligious views of death.

There were pressures from within the industry as well. Funeral corporations were purchasing the traditional family-owned or independent one-owner funeral homes. These large groups also purchased cemeteries, built crematories, and encouraged one-stop shopping. Even independent firms began to move to a multi-location configuration. In the same way that doctors and lawyers formed clinics or law partnerships, the advent of the group began to alter the funeral service environment.

Corporate thinking brought innovative, modern marketing plans, sales strategies, and distribution ideas. It also increased competition in a traditional low-key industry focused on dignity and even solemnity.

The public attitude was changing, the industry was changing, and the world was changing. The key to survival was to adapt and the funeral service industry has responded. To understand and illustrate some of those changes, here are examples of changes that have occurred since I first began in the profession.

Embalming

Every body, with very few exceptions, used to be embalmed. This was standard practice. We never asked permission, and only bodies being investigated for medical or legal reasons were exempt. We did not charge for embalming as it was considered part of the overall basic service we provided. Once in a while we would be advised that a family did not wish embalming, but that was very rare. Embalming accomplished three major objectives of the funeral director: sanitation, preservation, and beautification. It also fit the requirements for public viewing in an open casket.

Today, few bodies are automatically embalmed. There is also an added charge for the procedure. There is no legal requirement to embalm, and aside from a requirement for certain shipping situations it is not necessary. It has gone from a standard procedure to an option, and you as a consumer have been given a choice. The increasing use of cremation as an alternative to burying has also reduced the need for embalming.

Cremation

It is difficult to believe that in most cases in the past, other than in large cities, cremation was not available. Burial was the final disposition of choice. To have a body cremated, it had to be shipped, usually by rail, to a crematory in a distant location. As a funeral director, it really had little to do with the services I provided. It meant that instead of the hearse going to the cemetery, it went to railway station. I contacted the crematory and did the necessary paperwork, but it certainly didn't add or detract from my costs or profit.

In preparing this book, which is based on an in-depth review of present funeral industry practices, the increase in cremations has been the biggest surprise of all. One Canadian funeral home in Toronto states that in 1970 only 5 percent of families chose cremation. In 2000, more than 50 percent chose cremation. I will explain the process, the costs, and the advantages in a later chapter, but the option of cremation created by the expansion of available crematories has allowed the consumer a wider range of nontraditional choices.

Prearranged Funerals

The concept of dealing with death prior to need was virtually unheard of in the past. The public was not interested in investigating the consequences, financial or emotional, of this final event. It was, in fact, high on the list of taboos. People assumed that when the time came, you would learn all you needed to know. Some people felt that the discussion of death and funerals invited these events to arrive more quickly. The age of individual knowledge concerning health, social, sexual, and legal matters had not yet dawned. Death was discussed as a social event but never investigated as a business transaction.

There is still some resistance to the subject, but with the growth of the self-help and do-it-yourself industries, all life situations are questioned, and death and the final disposal of human remains is becoming an important part of estate, retirement, and financial planning. The baby-boom generation is now burying its parents and has made discussion of the subject a legitimate and important step in dealing with long-term issues. This generation operates on knowledge as the basis for good decision making, and funeral planning is becoming a natural part of that approach to modern living.

The funeral industry, after initial mistrust of the concept, has now accepted it, and in most cases professional funeral-service providers are eager to discuss options and choices with the public. Planned funerals are a very positive development for the public. Cost is one of the major factors that seem to be of interest. Prearranging allows the gathering of knowledge and a comparison of goods and services provided by a variety of sources. It allows the time to discuss your findings with loved ones or the person who will be in charge of your affairs. Most important, it can be conducted in an environment that is not charged with emotion or crisis, which is so often the case at the time of death. Many predict that within the next ten years as many as 50 percent of funerals will be prearranged.

Memorial and Commemorative Services

I have explained that a funeral is really a number of steps in a process, but to many, the word "funeral" denotes the gathering of family and friends for a memorial or commemorative service. In the past many or most would be held in a religious institution, but the funeral industry began building chapels in their establishments, and that became the standard location for most funerals in the past 40 years.

Those services and their locations are part of the changing face of our funeral practices. In my location, church services are the minority, chapel services are still the norm, and services now termed celebrations of life are conducted not only in funeral homes but also in many other locations. A recent funeral that I attended of a personal and business friend was held in a large conference room of a downtown hotel. It was conducted by friends and family, and no funeral home personnel were in attendance. The urn containing the cremated remains was present and was placed beside a frame of pictures depicting highlights of his life. The music was nonreligious but appropriate, and there were a few vases of flowers. I found it to be very personal, intimate, and in keeping with his views and personality. The family had made choices from options that were not possible or considered proper in the past.

Another option that seems to be growing is the choice of having no service at all. There are a number of reasons for this approach, which I will discuss further in Chapter 4.

Corporate Ownership

The funeral industry is a business that offers services and goods in a professional manner. Traditionally, funeral homes have been sole proprietorships or family businesses, and the industry and the public expected a professional standard of conduct as well as continuity in ownership and level of service.

This family ownership tradition has been challenged over the years, and a number of large corporations have purchased not only funeral homes but also cemeteries and crematories as well.

The five largest funeral-home corporations in the United States conduct 18 percent of the funerals and account for 20 percent of the annual revenues. The US holdings of the four major funeral-home chains include approximately 3,100 funeral homes and more than 1,000 cemeteries.

The public, however, does not seem to be too concerned about the ownership issue but are focused, rather, on value for money and a high standard of service, regardless of the funeral provider. The public seems more interested in a wide but good range of options, and people are increasingly using their ability to make wise and knowledgeable choices based on competition.

Professional Standards

In 1953, I graduated from the Canadian School of Embalming in Toronto, Ontario. It was conducted under the auspices of a Licensing Board and was affiliated with the University of Toronto. At that time it was the only school of its kind in Canada. Educational and training requirements had only recently been put in place in many Canadian provinces. I looked seriously at two embalming schools in the United States, but these were privately run and operated and they set their own course content. Today, most states and provinces have licensing requirements that demand a high quality of training and service.

Funeral service associations in both countries and other organizations are dedicated to offering the public the most honest, professional, and open representation possible.

Other changes in the funeral-service industry have occurred, including the growth of memorial societies. The funeral industry continues to evolve, driven by the changing views, perceptions, and needs of its customers. I believe that this is a healthy and positive environment for the purchaser of funeral services both now and in the future.

4
THE THREE STEPS TO FUNERAL PLANNING

Death presents us with two basic challenges. The first is physical and deals with the disposition of the body or human remains. There are the immediate tasks of making arrangements, fulfilling legal and other requirements, and seeing to the final disposition of the remains. Two of the three steps to full funeral planning deal with the physical requirements.

The second challenge is spiritual and emotional and is for the benefit of those we leave behind. For that reason, we hold services so that the grief stricken may deal with their sense of loss. Death leaves loved ones with a deep emotional wound and under a high degree of stress. Rituals and services are designed to acknowledge the life that has ended, and to promote both closure and healing for those left behind.

Many people think of a funeral as the remembrance portion of the three-step process that we must complete as part of the full funeral process. Much of this book is dedicated to informing you about the wide range of options available from the modern funeral industry. Based on those options, you can choose the type of funeral, the approximate cost of that funeral, and the people that you wish to be in charge of the process.

Your decisions will be based on having all the facts and discussing them with others. You will understand how your decisions will impact those that you leave behind. You can be assured that your funeral is cost-effective and reflects how you lived your life.

The three steps in the funeral process:

1. Choice of a funeral home

2. Service of Remembrance (optional)

3. Final disposition (cremation or burial)

Step 1: Immediate Disposition

No matter the place, the circumstances, or the degree of surprise, a tremendous emotional impact is felt the moment you accept the inevitability of death. Whether the death is sudden and unexpected or comes at the end of a long life or a valiant struggle with illness, the final pronouncement is a shock. It is at that moment or shortly after that the person(s) in charge of the deceased's affairs must answer the first question in the funeral process, "Where should we send the body?"

Regardless of the other choices, the body is usually sent to a funeral home. Even if you choose to have an immediate disposition with no service, there are still legal and other requirements. In 99 percent of cases in North America, a funeral home is the next step after the pronouncement of death. Even if you choose a memorial society, it will direct you to the funeral home that is contracted to deal with their funerals. If you have planned your funeral in advance of your death, your next-of-kin will already have the answer to the question. That answer will affect all the other decisions that are involved in the other two steps of the process. In the past your answer may have been motivated by tradition.

Your family may have ties to a particular funeral home because it always buried your family. Years ago the religion or ethnicity of the majority of its clients identified certain funeral homes. In other cases you may be acquainted with the owner or a member of the staff. Familiarity is always comforting in times of crisis or stress.

You may decide that the traditional family funeral home may or may not fit your needs and attitudes. On the other hand that same funeral home may have changed its options and attitudes since your last contact with them. Statistics show that most families experience a death in the family every 12 years.

When you have chosen your funeral professional, he or she will assist you in those necessary matters to progress to the second and third steps. Those details usually include —

- removal from the place of death to a funeral home, including storage of the body prior to final disposition; and

- an arrangement conference to gather information to secure the Medical Certificate of Death, the registration of death, cremation or burial permits, and official death certificates.

Note: This first step may carry a specific price or may be included with a package of services.

Choosing a funeral home

The choice of a funeral home and the funeral director that represents that establishment is extremely important. That choice should be based on such questions as the following:

- Do you know the establishment or the staff?

- Have you or others you know dealt with them and been satisfied?
- What is their standing in the community and how long have they been there?
- Does the funeral home and its staff hold valid licenses?
- Will they provide an itemized price list?
- Do they offer all of the services that you require?
- If you choose a memorial society, do you have the contact information for the funeral home that handles the society's business?

A funeral director has a multifaceted job. He or she is primarily a caregiver. Like a doctor, lawyer, or any other professional, a funeral director offers you advice, direction, and the benefit of his or her knowledge, training, and experience to guide you through the funeral. The funeral director is also an administrator and deals with all the necessary paperwork. Finally, remember that he or she is also a salesperson. In that capacity, the funeral director should be sympathetic to your priorities and wishes rather than acting as an aggressive advocate of the services or goods offered by the funeral home. That balance is the sign of professionalism that we should all expect and is also the goal of all funeral-service associations and regulating bodies of the funeral industry. The funeral-service associations set the standards, but it is the consumer who must be satisfied that these standards are met. Do not hesitate to ask questions or express your concerns at any time during the process.

Planning allows you to meet several potential funeral providers and choose the right individual or establishment you would prefer.

Every purchase made by a consumer presents an opportunity to the unscrupulous, unprofessional, or unprincipled supplier of goods and services. The funeral industry is no exception but its standards are high and an informed public is the best watchdog.

Information gathering

The major administrative tasks occur during the first step of the funeral process. These include the registration of death and the preparation of all required documents for burial or cremation. The death announcements, obituaries, and release of funeral service details are important and must be completed in this phase.

Once again, planning in advance of death allows time to gather information about the person for whom the funeral is being arranged. If it is for your own funeral, you may be the only one who knows some of that information.

Often documents such as birth, marriage, and divorce certificates, or other significant records must be located. Military-service records, as well as family connections, can be recorded and if necessary verified. Your funeral director can guide you through these informational and registration requirements, but both time and effort will be saved if you prepare the documents and include them as part of your funeral plan.

A full Biographical Information Sheet (see Appendix A) gives you an idea of the necessary information and will help you complete the

A cautious and informed purchaser should never be afraid to ask questions.

arrangements. It is a good idea to occasionally update this information after you complete your original funeral plan.

Basic information required immediately is shown below.

Information Required for Registration of Death

Full Name: _____

Address: _____

City: _____ State/Province: _____

Zip/Postal Code: _____

Home Phone Number: _____

Birth Date (month, day, year): _____

Birthplace (city, state/province): _____

Social Security/Social Insurance Number: _____

_____

_____

Marital Status (single, married, widowed, divorced): _____

_____

Spouse's Full Name: _____

Social Security/Social Insurance Number: _____

Spouse's Birth date (month, day, year): _____

Marriage Date and Location: _____

_____

_____

Father's Full Name: _____

Father's Birth Date (month, day, year): _____

Mother's Full Name: _____

Mother's Birth Date (month, day, year): _____

Step 2: Commemorative or Memorial Services

The second step in the funeral process involves the remembrance of the person and the life that he or she lived. In the past, almost every funeral had a religious focus. To conduct a funeral without a member of the clergy was rare, and there was a definite emphasis on the afterlife. When interviewing funeral directors for this book, I was surprised that the religious focus has diminished remarkably in the past 40 years. In my era, the religious involvement, even for nonchurchgoers was about 90 percent. I recently learned that religious involvement in my community is now about 15 percent. This finding may not apply in your community. There has been, however, a significant change in attitude towards funeral services.

Funerals are for the living

Funerals are not held or designed for the dead; they meet the needs and offer solace and comfort to the living. Remember this when you plan your funeral. At the beginning of this chapter, I said that death presents us with two distinct problems. The first, the immediate disposition of the body, is relatively simple; but the second, dealing with the emotional impact of a death, is much more complicated. One comment I have heard often while planning funerals in advance of a death is, "When I die, dump my body in a cheap box and get rid of it the simplest and cheapest way possible." The problem with this approach is that it does not take into consideration the feelings of those who are left behind. Humans need to mourn, grieve, and pay their last respects. They need to share their sense of loss and to offer comfort and support. These are important considerations and should not be dismissed lightly.

Funeral services are not conducted for the dead. They are designed to comfort and deal with the emotions of the living.

Allowing for grief

Commemorative or remembrance services are methods that have been used for centuries to deal with grief. Before discussing the design of any remembrance service, it might be helpful to examine the phenomenon of grief.

Grief is a normal emotional reaction to loss. The loss can be that of an article, a friend, a job, or a marriage. Death of a loved one is ranked as the number one most stressful event in human life. The stress varies depending on the depth of the relationship, but it is always considerable.

Shock is the first stage of grief, and even in the case of an expected death, an element of shock occurs. Sudden, unexpected, or traumatic death increases the shock level and the loss of a child is the most agonizing event that parents can imagine.

After the death and the funeral, there is often a sense of loneliness, isolation, and depression. Many people experience physical symptoms associated with depression. They can also feel anger and even guilt. These emotions are normal and part of the recovery process but, should they continue, it is wise to seek help.

Funeral services need not be depressing and mournful. In the past, the color black symbolized death; today the color is no longer associated with death and mourning.

Grief is a natural emotion. It is painful but a natural part of the process of acknowledging and coping with the loss of a loved one.

Many religions see death as a joyful entrance into the afterlife and an affirmation of spiritual beliefs.

The gathering of family, friends, and colleagues to share their loss, comfort each other, and celebrate the life of the deceased is a positive step when dealing with death.

Services of remembrance: Modern versus traditional

The memorial or commemorative service is the most involved, complicated, and expensive service. One of the major problems facing today's funeral industry is that, based on the traditional funeral culture many funeral providers invested in large and elaborate facilities complete with chapels and viewing rooms that focused on having an embalmed body open to public viewing in a casket. Today, more people are moving in the opposite direction and prefer a closed casket or a container designed only for burial or cremation. A service may include cremated remains in a small urn or no body or ashes present. It may take the form of a gathering of friends and family in any location and with a secular rather than religious remembrance service. These options reflect the public's change of attitude in dealing with death. Today's memorial service is more diverse, simple and, as a result, is less expensive.

Perhaps the best way to show the difference between a traditional funeral and the modern approach would be to describe the former and to show the options and choices now available in the latter.

With a traditional funeral, you paid for all the services whether or not you used them. The price, however, was solely determined by your choice of casket. Today, you may buy a preset package of traditional services or you may choose services and goods individually to form your own personally designed package.

The traditional funeral of the past

The normal sequence of arrangements was as follows:

1. The body was removed from the place of death and automatically embalmed, unless a rare nonembalming order was given to the funeral director.

2. The family attended a first conference with the funeral director, which was held in either the family home or at the funeral home.

3. All information was collected to facilitate the completion of the required documents for a certificate of death and a burial or cremation permit. Cremation was usually available only in large centers.

4. Newspaper notices and obituaries were written by the funeral home and released to the appropriate newspapers or radio stations.

5. Clothes were obtained and the body was dressed, cosmetics applied, and prepared for placement in a casket.

6. The person(s) responsible chose a casket and may have added an outer container to be placed in the grave (a wooden box, or a concrete or metal vault).

7. The body was placed in a viewing room or chapel for public or private visitation.

8. The family met with clergy to plan the program of the service.

9. Final arrangements were made with the family for such details as the placement of people in the church or the funeral cortege, disposition of flowers after the funeral, return of valuables on the body, and final check of pallbearers' names.

10. The funeral register was delivered to the home, if necessary, along with the acknowledgment cards.

Modern service options

A full service funeral today may follow the same sequence, but past assumptions are no longer valid:

1. *Embalming was automatic.*

   Bodies are no longer embalmed automatically. There is an extra charge if they are embalmed.

2. *Obituaries detailing the deceased's life, survivors, etc., were given to newspapers as news items.*

   Obituaries are not automatic and do not usually tell the deceased's life history, nor is there a post-funeral announcement describing the service, pallbearers, and out-of-town attendees. In large urban centers, obituaries can be very expensive.

3. *Burial was the choice of final disposition, as cremation was only available in large cities and transportation to a crematorium was difficult and expensive.*

   Burial is no longer the only or major means of final disposition, and in many areas, cremation is now the method of choice. Cremation eliminates many of the requirements of the traditional funeral. It does not require a casket, only a container. A grave or monument does not need to be purchased, and a graveside service or transportation of the body and funeral cortege to a cemetery is not required.

4. *Funeral services were held for every death even if only the funeral director and clergy were in attendance.*

   Immediate disposition by direct cremation or burial is becoming more common for various reasons. It eliminates cost of all services and goods necessary in a traditional funeral. In modern society, people are living longer, and families are not as close or as involved as in the past.

5. *Funerals were normally held in churches and later in funeral chapels.*

   The family, without the assistance of a funeral director, may hold a public or private funeral service in any appropriate location.

6. *Every funeral demanded the use of a casket for the body.*

   Many funerals are held today without the body being present. Public viewing is no longer necessary or expected. As a result, a casket and the preparation of the body, including embalming, cosmetics, and dressing, may not be necessary. If viewing is requested, a casket may be rented.

One of the main purposes of this book is to allow you to personally design the type of commemorative service you would prefer. Using the worksheets at the back of the book, you can state your preferences. You may make personal choices from a variety of options:

- Religious or nonreligious
- Public or family only, viewing or no viewing
- Location of the service
- Details concerning flowers, music, the order of service, and even after the post-funeral gathering

Funeral service options

Popular options for remembrance services include the following:

- *Religious:* This type of funeral may follow the rituals and ceremonies of any religion or particular denomination of a religion. The funeral may be held in a place of worship or funeral chapel and is characterized by the emphasis on the beliefs of the deceased concerning the afterlife. A clergyman usually conducts the service, and there can be prayers, readings, and music.

- *Nonreligious:* A semiformal service conducted by family or friends prior to or after final disposition. It highlights the personality, history, and remembrances of the deceased. This may be held in any location with the body present (a commemorative service) or without the body present (memorial service.) The service usually highlights various speakers and may or may not have music or readings. This service is often called a celebration of life, and pictures, mementos, and memorabilia may be shown.

- *Family gathering:* An informal gathering any time after final disposition. It can be held in any location and focuses on remembrance of the deceased as part of the family circle. There is no formal program. It may also occur when the ashes are scattered.

- *Private service:* Any type of service that limits the attendance to members of the family and invited guests.

- *Graveside service:* The service is held at the graveside or the place of the final disposition rather than gathering at a church, chapel, or other facility.

Step 3: Final Disposition

Final disposition of the remains may be by burial on land, burial at sea, or cremation.

Burial on land

Although cremation has grown in popularity over the past 30 years, burial is still final disposition of choice for most people in North America. Almost 75 percent in the United States and 58 percent in Canada choose burial over other options.

Some people argue that we are running out of space in cemeteries. This may be true in the urban centers but space exists to continue burials in smaller centers or in rural areas. For some people, there is a family plot or a cemetery containing the remains of family members. You will find more information about burial in Chapter 6 and Chapter 7.

Burial at sea

For centuries, burial at sea was a necessity as well as a ritual. A slow ship is no place to keep a decomposing body, especially in warmer climates.

Today, traditional burial at sea has taken on a new and innovative approach. With the increase in cremations, some people request their remains be scattered on water. This is an established practice in cremation. However, it is now possible for a body to be buried at sea, as in the past, or to inter remains in an urn or special biodegradable container and cast these into the sea.

There are special burial-at-sea services on both coasts of North America. Areas of sea bottom have been set aside for these urns and, in time, form part of an artificial reef. The cost is considerably lower than ground burial options.

There are three major types of service:

- *Witnessed:* Family or friends may accompany the remains for a committal service. The coordinates of the site are given so that the site may be revisited.
- *Unwitnessed:* The captain and crew make the committal.
- *Aerial dispersal:* An unaccompanied flight during which ashes are scattered at sea at least three miles from shore.

The United States Navy Mortuary Affairs conducts programs from six different centers. These burials at sea are performed on US Navy vessels while they are deployed and, therefore, family members are not permitted to attend the committals. The date, time, and the longitude and latitude of the committal are relayed to the family. A burial flag is required. Additional details can be found on the US Navy Web site under "Burial at Sea."

Cremation

I stated earlier that of all the changes in North American funeral practices over the past 50 years, the increase in cremation is the most dramatic. When I graduated from Embalming School in 1953, cremation statistics in the United States and Canada were:

	United States	Canada
1953	4%	2%

The latest statistics from the Cremation Association of America show a dramatic increase in less than 50 years.

	United States	Canada
1998	26%	45%

Cremation Statistics — United States

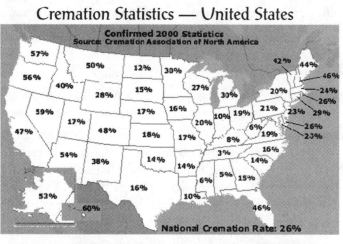

Cremation Statistics — Canada

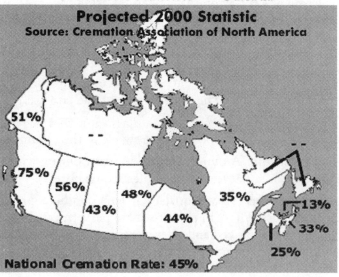

These figures show a strong shift in public attitudes toward cremation. Cremation has long been the choice for many other parts of the world. Available statistics from Japan (97 percent), Great Britain (70 percent), and Scandinavia (65 percent), show a preference for cremation over burial. In North America a number of factors have contributed to the rising popularity of cremation:

- The potentially lower cost

- Changing personal and spiritual beliefs

- Simplicity and convenience

- Acceptance by many religions

- Environmental concerns

- Dispersed families with no central family location

Choosing cremation does not alter the possibilities of friends and families conducting services, but reduces the focus on the physical presence of a body at those services. All options for remembrance remain open.

Chapter 7, dedicated to costs, shows the cost comparisons between burial and cremation. Cremation does offer potentially greater savings on the total cost of a funeral. The purchase of a casket, burial vault, cemetery plot, and grave opening and closing charges can be eliminated, and even if a monument is bought, it is usually smaller and less expensive.

The casket is the major merchandise purchase involved in a traditional funeral or funeral with a burial. Even if you choose viewing and body preparation as part of your funeral plan you can, in many funeral homes, now rent a casket. This type of casket is exactly the same as a regular casket, but the body is placed in a liner. When the viewing or service has been completed, the end of the casket is removed and the body and the liner slide out. This liner can then be placed in a cremation container and the casket returns to the display room of the funeral home. This rental casket concept is one of the newest and most unusual innovations in funeral merchandising and marketing.

Remember that many family members may be uncomfortable with the idea of cremation. Understand and acknowledge this while making your own preference known.

There is also a small but growing preference for direct disposal with no remembrance service. This can be done with a burial but is more common with cremation. Once the body is cremated, the question of disposition of the ashes still remains. A number of options exist:

- Burial (in some cases this may be done in a plot already containing a body)

- Placing the urn in a columbarium

- Placing an urn in a residence

- Scattering the ashes

Five reasons for choosing cremation:

1. Less expensive than burial

2. Environmental concerns

3. Simpler and less emotional

4. Dislike of burial

5. Ashes can be divided or strewn

Ashes may be scattered but there are legal and etiquette considerations.

Cremation frees the remains to be dealt with in ways that are not possible when the body is retained in its original form. Ashes need not be scattered or spread in one specific spot. Ashes may even be divided among family members if so desired. They can also be retained or distributed at different locations. Many people now leave specific instructions regarding the scattering of their ashes.

Ash scattering may be the most popular method of final disposition, and I am amazed at the unique and often unusual places chosen to scatter ashes. The ashes can be placed somewhere that was important to the deceased. This is yet another form of remembrance. Ashes may also be buried in a container. My parents are buried in a three-grave plot purchased more than 20 years ago. Recently, while visiting the site, I inquired at the office to check that the plot was now registered in my name and confirmed that there was still one space for committal. I was surprised to learn that in fact there were seven spaces available: one for burial of a body and two for burials of cremated remains in each of the three plots. For those who own plots with existing burials, this is a worthy point and should be investigated. In my case, should I or any of my family choose cremation, the benefits would include —

- no need to buy a new plot,
- reduced opening and closing charges,
- no need for a casket or burial vault, and
- the opportunity for more family members to be buried in one location.

These points now become factors in planning my funeral statement on final disposition. It should also be noted that ashes are purified and therefore pose no environmental hazard.

5
RESPONSIBILITIES AND REQUIREMENTS

Because of the emotional factors involving death, there is always the possibility of disagreement over the person with the authority to make funeral arrangements. The executor of the deceased's will, if not a family member, will often allow or even encourage family members to get involved in the decision-making process.

Who Has the Power to Act?

As there is always the possibility of disagreements within families regarding funeral arrangements, the following guidelines are generally accepted. Note, however, that laws may vary depending on your jurisdiction.

Who controls the disposition of the human remains? The order of priority should be as follows:

1. The person named in the legal will as the personal representative of the deceased. This person is usually referred to as the executor.

2. If living with the deceased at the time of death, the spouse of the deceased. This may include a common-law spouse.

3. An adult child of the deceased. In the case of more than one child, the order of priority begins with the eldest child and descends in order of age.

4. A parent of the deceased.

Choose a proper executor for your will and a reliable person to carry out your funeral plan. Share with them your wishes, preferences, and expectations.

5. An adult brother or sister of the deceased.

6. An adult nephew or niece of the deceased.

7. Any other next of kin, as defined by law.

If anyone in this descending order is unwilling or unable to assume control, the right passes to the next available qualified person.

Funeral-service providers should not provide burial or cremation arrangements unless written authorization is received from the person in control of the disposition.

The Duties of the Person in Control

The following is a list of tasks that need to be carried out when someone dies. Not all the tasks must be done immediately, but all have a bearing on the final disposition of the deceased's remains and his or her affairs. Many people are not aware of the duties of an executor. Not all of the duties listed below necessarily fall to this person. If an executor is a different person than the spouse, the executor may feel that the spouse could carry out a number of these duties. Cooperation and sensitivity are important.

Decisions and tasks

- Assemble personal information
- Locate important documents
- Arrange funeral-service details
- Decide participants
- List people to contact
- Compile costs

People and agencies to contact

- Immediate family, including estranged members, should be considered
- Close friends
- Employer
- Accountant
- Lawyer
- Life insurance company
- Veteran's affiliation
- Banks and other financial institutions
- Post office

Information required for registrations

- Full legal name
- Address

- Date of birth
- Place of birth
- Date of marriage
- Full name of spouse
- Next of kin
- Occupation
- Doctor's name and address

Documents and papers

- Most current legal will
- Written funeral plan
- Prepaid funeral plan, owned cemetery plots, or funeral insurance
- Birth certificates of the deceased and dependents
- Marriage certificate(s)
- Divorce papers
- Citizenship papers
- Medical benefit cards
- Passport
- Bank or credit institution documents, passbooks, and credit cards
- Previous two years' income tax returns
- Stocks, bonds, or shares
- Insurance policies: life, home, contents, and car
- Deeds, mortgages, and loan details
- Car, recreational vehicle, or boat-ownership papers
- Private, employment, and government pension details
- Social Security Number (United States) or Social Insurance Number (Canada)
- Records of any benefits: government, disability, or veterans
- Professional, association, and club membership fees or dues
- Outstanding contracts
- Bills

Funeral-service decisions and special instructions

- Traditional funeral home or memorial society
- Time, location, and date of service
- Open or closed casket, private or public viewing
- Pallbearers (active and/or honorary)
- Instructions regarding jewelry, clothing, and embalming and preparation

- Clergy, scripture, readings, music, organist, hymns, eulogy, or speakers
- Floral tributes or memorial donations to charity
- Arrangement for refreshments and gathering of friends after the service
- Thank-you cards, book of remembrance, and photographs

Obituary information
- Family members to be named
- Educational information
- Employment history
- Accomplishments, awards, or medals
- Hobbies and special interests
- Clubs, lodges, or organization memberships

Death Is a Legal Matter

The four major life events of birth, marriage, divorce, and death all carry legal implications. Of the four, death is the most complicated and most legally controlled. The keeping of records and official documents of death reach far back in our history and are an important part of the funeral rite.

As with birth, marriage, and divorce, a certificate must mark the event of a death. The death certificate is usually a combination of two forms used to register the death with the appropriate authorities. One form outlines the vital statistics concerning the deceased, including all personal information such as name, address, age, and place of birth. This clearly defines the identity of the deceased. The second form is a medical statement completed by the attending or family physician. In the case of police involvement, it might be necessary that the coroner sign the medical statement, which states the cause of death. The coroner is called and attends in those situations that are deemed medical/legal, such as death by violence (murder, suicide, and motor-vehicle accident) or in any circumstances in which the police authorities might suspect foul play.

The two documents are registered and a death certificate is issued. This is necessary for all legal transactions concerning the death, such as applications for burial or cremation, and insurance and other claims. All require proof of death, and the death certificate is the most recognized and accepted document.

In addition to the death certificate, there are many other permissions and requirements to deal with. The person legally responsible for these matters should be aware of their legal responsibilities and restrictions.

The list below summarizes situations that require the authorization of an executor, next of kin, or person of authority:

Death is a legal matter.

- *Autopsy permission:* The attending physician or the hospital in which the death occurred may request an autopsy. This is an extensive examination of the body and is usually performed soon after death. You may decline the request. The only time permission is not required to perform an autopsy is if a coroner orders one to establish cause of death.

- *Body or organ donation:* Both of these bequests must be approved and have signed releases.

- *Contracts after death:* The funeral director and all goods and service providers supplying the funeral will require authorization and assurance of payment. Family members or friends should not be involved in the contracting of these items unless authorized to do so or they may be held liable for payment.

- *Cemetery and cremation facilities:* Both of these facilities have legal requirements and need authorization to perform their respective duties. A body may not be cremated until 48 hours after death.

The Funeral Rule and Other Consumer Safeguards

In 1984, the United States Federal Trade Commission developed a regulation concerning funeral-industry practices. It is called the Funeral Rule and is designed to guarantee that consumers have free and honest access to information concerning funeral arrangements.

These regulations deal with such items as —

- telephone price disclosures,
- the general price list,
- embalming information,
- cash advance sales,
- caskets for cremation,
- required purchase of unwanted goods,
- a statement of funeral goods or services selected including the total price,
- preservative and protective claims, and
- other considerations.

To obtain full information about the Funeral Rule or specific information relating to your state, you should contact the State Licensing Board or the Conference of Funeral Service Examining Board, 520 E. Van Tees Street, P.O. Box 497, Washington, IN 47501, telephone

(812) 254-7887. You can also obtain additional information from the Funeral Rule Web site (www.ftc.gov/bcp/conline/pubs/buspubs/funeral.htm).

In Canada there is no such universal rule, but as a consumer you are protected, as with any other purchase by federal, provincial, and even municipal laws that apply to purchases of goods and services.

Should you have concerns or questions about any matter, you should contact the governing body of funeral affairs in your state or province.

6
FUNERAL PROVIDERS

Many specialized companies and businesses provide both goods and services to the funeral industry. Some of these include —

- funeral homes,
- memorial societies,
- cemeteries,
- crematories,
- casket, container, and vault companies,
- embalming and supply companies,
- funeral equipment furnishing companies,
- hearse and automotive companies,
- funeral stationery suppliers, and
- monument companies.

There are also providers that offer products and services in addition to those used for funerals. These include —

- clergy,
- florists, and
- organists.

A description of the major providers — funeral homes, memorial societies, cemeteries, and crematories — is included in this chapter.

Choose your funeral director with an eye to reputation, standing in the community, and word-of-mouth satisfaction. A satisfied customer is still the most reliable advertisement.

Funeral Homes

The major funeral provider is the funeral home. Until recently, it provided professional advice on all matters pertaining to funerals with the exception of cemetery and cremation services. In the past, funeral homes were not allowed to own or operate cemeteries or crematories. The modern funeral home now provides not only traditional goods and services but also operates cemeteries and crematories.

Many funeral homes have all three options on one site or located in the same area or city. Many now sell urns, memorial markers, funeral stationery, and other items of merchandise in addition to caskets and burial vaults.

The funeral director

The funeral director is a licensed, trained, and experienced counselor, guide, and caregiver, and deals directly with you on every aspect of the funeral arrangements.

Here are a few of the services provided:

- The funeral director will conduct an initial interview to get information about the deceased so that the death can be registered and necessary permits obtained. That information will contain at least 20 legal facts, and a number of signatures are necessary for registration and permits.
- He or she will begin arrangements for final burial or cremation.
- He or she will discuss the funeral ceremony and all details pertaining to it (clergy or master of ceremonies, flowers, music, pallbearers' seating, ceremony seating arrangements for family, cars, and parking).
- He or she will explain possible death benefits (government, veterans, etc.).
- He or she will write and distribute obituaries and funeral notices.
- He or she will provide the staff, facilities (chapel and viewing rooms), and equipment (cars, hearse) based on your choices.
- He or she will explain all details concerning purchases (caskets, vaults, liners, urns, and monuments).
- He or she will offer funeral financing plans or other options for payment.
- He or she will return personal effects including jewelry.
- He or she will handle the register and thank-you cards to family.

What does the funeral director and other funeral-home staff do?

Some job descriptions are easy to define. Even children know what doctors, teachers, and firefighters do, but some occupations are harder to define. Whenever I ask for the job descriptions of the funeral director and other funeral-home staff, I get answers like, "They handle dead people," or "They run funerals." When you pay someone to do a job, you should know what services to expect. Funeral-home staff, led by the funeral director, perform many and varied tasks on your behalf while conducting a traditional funeral. The words "professional services" on your account stand for the time and effort expended by the funeral-home staff and include the overhead costs that every business factors into its charges. For a list of services offered by funeral-home staff, see the side bar on this page.

The business establishment

Another cost-related factor is the size and style of the facility. Some funeral establishments are new and lavish; others are older and more modest. Prices may vary according to the size of the establishment, number of staff members, equipment, hearses, and other vehicles. As with any other business, these factors may affect the overall cost.

Memorial Societies

In the introduction, I stated that funeral practices in North America underwent major changes in the past 50 years. In the 1950s, the funeral industry offered its services through individual funeral homes in towns and cities. Either the funeral home was the only local service provider, or in the case of larger centers, a number of funeral homes competed for business.

The birth and growth of alternative approaches

Early in the last century, in the United States, organizations were formed to provide simple, dignified funeral options at the lowest possible costs. In the latter part of the 1950s, a protest movement grew, based on the belief that the funeral industry offered and promoted funerals that were too lavish and expensive. Two best-selling books, *The American Way of Death* by Jessica Mitford and *The High Cost of Dying* by Ruth Mulvey Harmer, fueled the protest against the funeral industry. The Unitarian Church was a leader among those who wanted to return to the simpler procedures of earlier days. A number of alternatives to the traditional funeral-home offerings grew from this discontent. The memorial society is one of the best known alternatives.

The individual duties and services provided by funeral-home staff are:

1. Professional consultation and advice on the funeral process, including knowledge of and adherence to legal requirements.

2. Completion of required registrations and documentation.

3. Administrative, public reception, and information duties related to the death and funeral.

4. Facilities, specialized equipment, and training for the removal, storage, preservation, and handling of human remains.

5. Hearses, furniture, and other equipment necessary for funerals.

6. Facilities designed for public funeral services and public or private viewing.

7. The display and sale of appropriate merchandise, including caskets, urns, vaults, funeral stationery, grave markers, etc.

What is a memorial society?

Memorial societies are nonprofit organizations run by a board of directors that is elected from the society's membership. The societies do not own or operate funeral homes, cemeteries, or crematories. The general purposes of these organizations are to promote dignity and simplicity in funeral rites; to arrange, before death, for its members and their families such lawful disposition of their remains as they desire; and to arrange memorial services. They also educate the public about funeral consumer concerns and alternatives and, finally, act as monitors of the industry and the legislation that affects it.

What does a memorial society offer?

A member of a memorial society can access the specific services of the licensed and professional funeral home contracted with the society for a specific price.

Packages vary, but as an example, they might offer the following different options:

1. *Immediate disposition:* This includes the transfer of the deceased from the place of death to the designated, contracted funeral home; arrangement conference with the next of kin or executor; completion and filing of necessary documents, including registration of death; and minimum-cost container for burial or cremation. It is at this point that the person(s) responsible for the funeral must make decisions about further steps, including final disposition by burial or cremation. The society's funeral home usually offers additional service packages at an additional price.

2. *Memorial service:* This option includes all of the items under immediate disposition, plus the use of the funeral chapel for religious or secular services (without the remains of the deceased present); staff for direction of service, and one vehicle to transport the family to and from the service. The family may arrange a memorial service or celebration of life gathering at a location of their choice without the need for funeral-home staff or vehicles. In this case, only the immediate-disposition charges (Option 1) would apply.

3. *Funeral service:* This option includes all items mentioned under immediate disposition, plus the use of the funeral home for a religious or secular service (with the deceased present in a closed casket) and with staff present to direct services in the funeral-home chapel or church, one vehicle to transport family to the service, and if burial is to follow, to the cemetery.

See Sample 1, "Memorial Society Options," for more information.

A simple graveside service might also be possible, which would include all the items mentioned under immediate disposition, plus staff attendance at the graveside, use of the funeral coach, and one vehicle to transport the family to and from the cemetery.

The cost of each package increases depending on the use of the funeral-home's staff, facilities, and equipment.

There are other items that are not included in the package of goods and services but which may be mandatory, necessary, or that you choose to add to complete the funeral. Necessary additional costs would include goods and services taxes applicable to your location, and fees for originals and duplicates of death certificates. The option that you choose for the final disposition of the body would be a necessary cost. The burial or cremation fees are separate and may or may not be services offered by your chosen funeral home. In the same manner, cremation fees, burial space, and opening and closing charges by a cemetery may have to be purchased from an independent source.

Making the most of your options

Membership in a memorial society that entitles you to the use of the contracted funeral home can meet all the stages of a complete funeral plan and a prepayment option.

Remember that when dealing with the society's contracted funeral home, you are dealing with a facility that probably offers the full service options of a traditional funeral home. If you deviate from that plan, your original decision to take advantage of the benefits of the society — dignity and simplicity at the lowest cost — may be jeopardized.

Cemeteries

In North America the traditional choice for final disposition has been burial in a cemetery. The word cemetery is derived from German and means a sleeping place. There are many kinds of cemeteries that vary from large and formal to very small. Some are beautifully landscaped and maintained; others are abandoned and forgotten. In our culture, they are all considered sacred. Some major cities in the United States have more than 200 cemeteries.

The basic types of cemeteries are —

- national (usually for veterans and are government controlled),
- public nonprofit (usually municipally owned and operated),
- religious nonprofit (exclusive to a religion or denomination), and
- commercial (owned and operated as a business for profit).

Cemeteries are strictly regulated and provide a rich history of our nation. Cemeteries account for the final whereabouts for most citizens in a way that the scattering of ashes cannot.

Should you choose burial for yourself or your family, be aware that it is a distinct segment of the full funeral process. As such, you should understand what burial entails and its related costs.

Burial carries significant costs. A cemetery plot and the other elements of burial — such as a vault, grave liner (a requirement in many

SAMPLE 1
MEMORIAL SOCIETY OPTIONS

OPTION 1	OPTION 2	OPTION 3
IMMEDIATE DISPOSITION	**MEMORIAL SERVICE**	**FUNERAL SERVICE**
* All items in Option 1, plus 1. Transference of diseased to funeral home 2. Arrangement conference with next of kin/executor 3. Completion and filing of necessary documents, including registration of death 4. Minimum cost container for burial or cremation	* All items in Option 1, plus 1. Use of funeral-home chapel for religious or secular service 2. Staff for direction of service (without deceased present) 3. Transportation (one vehicle) for family, to and from service	** All items in Option 1, plus 1. Use of funeral-home chapel for religious or secular service (with deceased present — closed casket) 2. Staff attendance to direct service in church or funeral home 3. One vehicle to transport family to and from funeral and cemetery, and return
$ 440.00 + recording fee $25.00	$ 710.00 + recording fee $25.00	$1,045.00 + recording fee $25.00
	Note: If family arranges the memorial service at their own location (church) and funeral-home staff are not required, only the charge for Option 1 applies.	**Note:** If pallbearers are used, the funeral home will supply one vehicle for transportation to and from location of service, to and from cemetery.
Not included 1. Goods and services tax 2. Cost of death certificates 3. Basic urn, cemetery costs, clergy honorariums, musicians, flowers, obituaries, embalming 4. Cremation fees 5. Transportation costs outside of 45 km (30 miles)	As in Option 1	As in Option 1

cemeteries), or monument — can equal or be more expensive than each of the other steps. Today, in large cities and in some commercial cemeteries, burial is very expensive.

Most cemeteries have perpetual-care or care-fund costs that may be billed either separately or as part of the cost of the plot. This means that the cemetery will maintain the gravesite into the future. A portion of your purchase cost is set aside to guarantee this maintenance.

Cemeteries have changed over the years. If you visit an older section of a cemetery, you can wander among a variety of headstones or statuaries. The modern cemetery usually has ground-level markers to allow machinery to keep the grounds maintained. Most cemeteries today also have provisions for the burial or entombment of the ashes of cremated remains.

When choosing a cemetery it is wise to consider questions such as the following:

- Are you purchasing the plot for yourself or will your spouse or other members of the family also wish to be buried there?
- Is the desire for religious or consecrated ground a factor?
- Would you prefer a central location, easily accessible to the majority of the family?
- Could unused spaces be sold later if not needed or wanted?

Cemetery visitation is much less popular than it was in the past, but there are still many who feel that the family cemetery plot is a special and important family focus point.

Crematories

In North America cremation is the second most popular method used for the final disposition of human remains. The term crematory refers to either the furnace or the structure in which the furnace is located. Originally crematories were separate entities, as were cemeteries but they are now often part of a one-stop shopping owned and operated by a funeral home or corporation.

The process of cremation is simple and dignified. It normally takes from 90 minutes to 3 hours and reduces the remains to approximately 3 to 9 pounds of purified bone fragments referred to as "ashes."

The usual steps in the cremation process are:

1. Individual remains enclosed in a suitable casket or container are placed in the furnace.
2. The furnace is heated to temperatures of over 1,400 degrees Fahrenheit.
3. The heat is maintained for a period of 90 minutes to 3 hours.
4. The body substances are consumed leaving bone fragments and all noncombustible material (dental gold, prosthesis material, casket metal including screws, nails, hinges, or latches).

Note: While remains may be cremated within 48 hours without any other services, this act of cremation is usually considered the final disposition (step 3) in the full funeral process.

5. The furnace is cooled.

6. The cremated remains and noncombustible items are removed.

7. The bone fragments (ashes) are placed in an appropriate container or urn.

8. The container is returned to the family or person designated to receive them.

Transportation

There are two main categories concerning the transportation of human remains. They are short-distance transportation and long-distance transportation. There is also a great deal of difference between transporting cremated remains in a small container and transporting a body.

In this era of travel and dispersed families, it is not unusual for a death to take place some distance from home. If you or a member of your family dies in another country, the return home of the body can be an involved and expensive consideration.

Once again, your funeral director can give you approximate costs for a funeral home's receiving and shipping services, but the cost of the actual transportation by air, rail, road, or water can vary significantly. There are also other considerations that may come into effect, such as regulations governing embalming and shipping-container requirements.

You cannot forecast all eventualities, but you might want to add these considerations to your funeral statements and plan. If you die in a foreign country or a long distance from your home, would you prefer to —

- not be returned home but have an immediate disposition at the place of death?

- be cremated at the place of death, if possible, and have your ashes returned by post or courier? or

- have your body returned in spite of cost?

If you die a short distance from home, the funeral director can usually work out the fastest, easiest, and most economical way to transfer the body. If your family has to deal with two funeral homes, there will be two charges. I recommend that your family contact your local funeral director to make the transfer arrangements rather than deal with the funeral home at the place of death.

7
FUNERAL COSTS

When you purchase funeral services, you should understand what you are buying. When you buy a car, a home, or any other item, you automatically question its quality, reliability, and cost. There seems to be a greater reluctance to question these factors when you purchase professional services. Purchases are based on needs or desires and can have a negative or positive and high or low emotional impact. The purchase of goods is normally pleasurable, but the purchase of services may include a negative and/or emotional factor. But there is no purchase that carries a higher risk of emotional and psychological impact than the purchase of a funeral.

The number one stress factor in life is the loss of a loved one. For this reason, the purchase of funeral services places you, as the consumer, in a position of vulnerability. Your first defense is knowledge. With this knowledge, you can understand and deal with your emotional needs so that your judgment isn't clouded when making a business decision.

Buyer Beware

Don't forget that a funeral home is a business. Cemeteries, crematories, and monument makers are all businesses. They are professional service providers, just like family doctors or lawyers. While funeral homes do provide professional advice in a number of areas, they are primarily commercial enterprises designed and operated for profit. The number of goods and services you choose will decide the profit of the funeral provider.

The wise shopper compares quality and price.

The bitterness of low quality remains long after the sweetness of low price is forgotten.

The funeral industry in the United States is estimated to take in 16 billion dollars per year. Due to the aging of the baby-boom generation, it is considered a growth industry.

In the past, the local funeral home has been a family name institution much the same way as a family doctor's practice. Continuity and tradition have been highly prized in the funeral profession. During the past 40 years, however, large conglomerates have purchased many local funeral homes, creating chain operations. Two examples are the Canada-based Loewen Group and, in the United States, the Houston-based Service Corporation International (SCI), which is reported to conduct 1 in every 9 funerals in the US. Estimates show that the conglomerates now own 20 percent of funeral homes, crematories, and cemeteries. Funeral-home chains are based on the concept that operating costs would be lower through efficient administration and volume purchase of merchandise items and the provision of various services. But it has been suggested by critics of the corporations that those savings are being passed on to the shareholder rather than the consumer.

The consumer of funeral goods and services, like any consumer of business products and services, should keep two basic warnings in mind: "Buyer beware" and "Protect yourself at all times."

The time to learn about this subject is before you are forced to do so. Comparison shopping today is a fact of life. You are bombarded daily by flyers, advertisements, and all manner of information that allows you to make choices based on your knowledge of the product. Whether it is groceries or a car, you can quickly find the lowest price for the same product or service. Traditionally, we do not comparison-shop for professional services. We assume that all professional service providers charge the same. However, the costs of specialized services offered by doctors, lawyers, dentists, financial planners, bankers, and real estate agents vary greatly. You may have the time to explore different options when buying a house or deciding on a car, but when a doctor or nurse tells you that your loved one is dead and wants to know where to send the body, you will not be in the emotional state to begin comparison shopping.

Be an informed and knowledgeable consumer and you will be better equipped to make sensible and rational choices when the need for funeral services arise. Each item you purchase such as a casket, an urn, or a cemetery plot has a variable cost. Each service offered, whether it is the preparation of documents, writing an obituary, embalming, the use of a chapel or vehicles, can be purchased individually or as a package. By understanding the emotional and financial aspects of these purchases, you are better prepared to make wise and satisfying decisions.

The perceived high cost of funerals has been a topic of discussion in books, magazine articles, and television documentaries over the past 40 years. A funeral can be expensive but it is as important as buying a house, a car, or any other item. You make the final decision on the cost. A full funeral can cost less than $1,000 and more than $10,000.

In addition to the high cost of certain goods such as caskets, vaults, and cemetery plots the real public concern is that the funeral industry, unlike a real estate agent or car dealer, is dealing with an emotionally vulnerable buyer. Knowledge of the funeral process and taking the step of planning your own funeral will reduce the emotional factor.

Every profession and business has horror stories of inflated prices, badly made merchandise, and poor customer service. Unethical practices appear to be rampant when reported in the media. The funeral industry has had, and continues to have, more than its share of bad press.

However, considering that in the United States there are 22,000 funeral homes dealing with 2.3 million deaths a year (not to mention that there are a further 200,000 deaths per year in Canada), the percentage of dissatisfied consumers is very low. The funeral industry, through its national, state, and provincial professional associations, strives to maintain a high degree of ethics, training, and reliable service. When you choose a funeral provider, choose someone whom you trust and who makes you feel comfortable.

When discussing funeral costs, the first task is to list all items individually. I have broken these down by category. When comparing costs, obtain quotes from the funeral providers on all the services and goods that you want. These include costs charged by the funeral home, cemetery, or crematory, and any other service provider. In some cases, one provider may offer all the goods and services, including cremation and cemetery charges, while others may offer only those they provide directly. Funeral homes often include third-party items shown as "other" on the invoice.

Remember to add the applicable taxes, as the funeral provider may not necessarily include these in the quote.

Be sure to consider the total cost of your funeral purchase. The total should include taxes and, if needed, extra death certificates.

Funeral-home charges

Transfers: This charge refers to the transportation of the body from one place to another and can include transfers to the funeral home from the place of death, to the crematory, the cemetery, or to a commemorative-service location.

Preparation: These charges usually refer to the sanitary care, dressing, or preparation of the body for either viewing or placement in a container for burial or cremation. There may also be a separate charge to remove a pacemaker.

Embalming: This procedure is usually a separate charge and must be requested. Additional charges may apply for restorative work that may be necessary if the deceased died by trauma or by an appearance-changing illness.

Staff: The use of staff is normally included in basic charges, but there are situations for which additional staff is required. These may include attendance at a cremation as a witness, attendance at a committal or scattering of remains, and staff time during day or evening visitation hours.

Facility use: Charges may be applicable for visitation time or a reception after the funeral.

Caskets: This item is usually the most costly on a funeral account. The term is used here to include caskets for viewing OR any container of any material used to hold the remains for burial or cremation.

Memorial stationary: This item includes memorial books, registers, and thank-you cards.

Burial or cremation charges

Cremation fees: This charge represents the cost of the cremation of a body already in a cremation container.

Packaging: There may be a packaging cost for shipping cremated remains.

Urn: The urn is any container that holds (either temporarily or permanently) the cremated ashes. Containers are usually made of plastic, wood, marble, metal, ceramic, or porcelain.

Grave: This item refers to the individual space allotted for burial or cremation. Other members of a family may purchase a number of adjoining graves for later use. This group of graves is referred to as a plot. Interment space can also be purchased for cremated remains or they may be placed in a niche in a columbarium. There is a separate cost for this.

Opening and closing charges: This charge is for labor and/or equipment necessary to complete the burial.

Vaults and liners: These are used to protect the casket or urn when placed in the ground. Some cemeteries insist on their use. They may be made of concrete, metal, or other types of long-lasting material.

Memorial markers

Memorials: These charges refer to any stone monuments, metal markers, or memorial trees. There is normally a cost for the memorial and a further cost for installation.

Shipping and transportation charges

Receiving or sending remains: Charges may be made for either sending or receiving a body to or from another destination. These arrangements and costs should be fully investigated prior to the actual shipment. There would also be a cost for short-distance travel, which could include vehicle use and staff time.

Other charges

- Death certificate(s)
- Memorial-society records fee

- Clergy honorarium
- Floral arrangements
- Organist
- Obituary notices

When funeral providers quote the charges for these goods and services, they may be described in a slightly different way. A number of goods and services are packaged in one price as outlined in the three basic types of charges (immediate disposition, memorial service, or traditional funeral). Compare all the items in the package to this full list.

Comparison Shopping

When buying a house or car, you look at a number of different options and compare the various features and prices. The same wise consumer behavior is necessary when making decisions on a funeral.

Funeral homes are required by law to answer your request for prices on all goods and services. Many people are reluctant to visit funeral homes to request quotes. They worry that they may be pressured by sales pitches to make premature decisions. If that happens, you will not be comfortable with that provider. Do not be afraid to tell them so. Know what your funeral preferences are before you shop for prices.

A funeral provider who will not give you information on the phone will leave a bad impression. One that will not give you prices in writing is breaking the law.

Sample costs

It would be almost impossible to illustrate cost comparison shopping in a way that would be relevant and accurate for all of North America. I suggest that you obtain costs from various funeral providers in your local area. The cost comparison charts in this guide are based on those I prepared for my funeral statement, and the quotes were provided by funeral-service providers in my community.

If you are reluctant or uncomfortable approaching a funeral home, cemetery or crematory, you can telephone and ask them to send you their price list. Or you can ask a friend or relative to collect the material from the funeral home.

Within my local area I was able to obtain prices from all types of funeral providers, including —

- a corporate-owned, full-service funeral home with an on-site cemetery and crematory;
- a sole-proprietor, one-location, full-service provider with a crematory;
- one of the largest memorial societies in North America and their contracted funeral home; and
- nonprofit cemeteries owned and operated by a municipality and religious denominations.

There are many options in choosing all segments of a funeral plan. You should discuss all of your options before making a final choice.

The Local Cost Comparison Charts (see Sample 2) illustrate my findings and provide a range of costs that you should encounter in your own community.

In comparing the prices, remember several points:

- It is very important that you have a clear idea from your funeral plan and statements what goods and services you wish to have priced. This information may be obtained over the phone, but for clarification, a visit to the service provider may be necessary. To properly compare casket costs, style, and quality you should examine them.

- Prices vary tremendously in different parts of the country, between small and large centers, and throughout North America. Get at least three quotes in your own area. (**Note:** This part of the comparison is similar to buying a car. Know the level and the type of model you want and can afford. Don't be swayed by options or packaging. Keep it simple.)

- When comparing funeral homes, don't concentrate only on price. The surroundings, amenities, equipment, staff, reputation, and overall feeling are all important. Is the funeral home open to your questions or are they more interested in their agenda?

- Finally, how would your family and friends be comforted in these surroundings? What is the attitude of the staff?

- If you prefer one funeral home and it is close in price to the lowest bid, don't be afraid to return and ask them to match the lower price. This is a very competitive industry.

The Cost Comparison Charts are also provided in blank form for your use in the worksheets section at the back of the book. Use these worksheets to gather information concerning the prices that you receive during your inquiries.

Note: The items listed in the Cost Comparison Charts are basic and may vary from one funeral home to another and may differ substantially based on your geographical location. The examples given are based on approximate figures obtained from funeral providers within my local and regional area. For exact services and costs in your location contact your local funeral homes or memorial societies.

After studying the charts, you will notice that there is a range of costs from high to low. None of the three providers quoted the same price. This is further evidence that you should obtain estimates prior to need. Note that within the services listed, a similar amount has been used for the purchase of the casket. You may not be able to match the quality and style of specific caskets. Funeral homes, like car dealerships, carry different models.

SAMPLE 2
IMMEDIATE DISPOSITION: Step 1
(Local Cost Comparison — Chart 1)

FUNERAL HOME A		MEMORIAL SOCIETY		FUNERAL HOME B	
Removal		Removal		Removal	
Facility use		Facility use		Facility use	
Arrangement conference		Arrangement conference		Arrangement conference	
Documentation & registration		Documentation & registration		Documentation & registration	
Body preparation	430.00	Body preparation	440.00	Body preparation	954.00
		Membership & recording fee	45.00		
Cremation cost	285.00	Cremation cost	305.00	Cremation cost	295.00
Container	30.00	Container	n/c	Container	68.00
Total	745.00	Total	790.00	Total	1,317.00

MEMORIAL SERVICE: Step 2 (A)
(No body or casket present)
(Local Cost Comparison — Chart 2)

FUNERAL HOME A		MEMORIAL SOCIETY		FUNERAL HOME B	
Removal		Removal		Removal	
Facility use		Facility use		Facility use	
Arrangement conference		Arrangement conference		Arrangement conference	
Documentation & registration		Documentation & registration		Documentation & registration	
Body preparation		Body preparation		Body preparation	
Use of funeral chapel		Use of funeral chapel		Use of funeral chapel or visitation room	
Staff for direction of services	1,150.00	Staff for direction of services	710.00	Staff for direction of services	
		Membership & recording fee	45.00	Professional service fee	2,039.00
PLUS		PLUS		PLUS	
Cremation	315.00	Cremation	305.00	Cremation	363.00
OR		OR		OR	
Cemetery charges		Cemetery charges		Cemetery charges	
(See Final Disposition Chart)		(See Final Disposition Chart)		(See Final Disposition Chart)	
Grand total	1,465.00	Grand total	1,060.00	Grand total	2,402.00

SAMPLE 2 — Continued
TRADITIONAL SERVICE: Step 2 (B)

(Local Cost Comparison — Chart 3)

FUNERAL HOME A		MEMORIAL SOCIETY		FUNERAL HOME B	
Removal		Removal		Removal	
Facility use		Facility use		Facility use	
Arrangement conference		Arrangement conference		Arrangement conference	
Documentation & reg.		Documentation & reg.		Documentation & reg.	
Body preparation		Body preparation		Body preparation	
Use of funeral chapel		Use of funeral chapel		Use of funeral chapel	
Staff direction of services		Staff direction of services		Staff direction of services	
Vehicles (3)	1,500.00	Vehicles (1)	1,045.00	Vehicles (3)	
				Professional fee	2,039.00
IN ADDITION		**IN ADDITION**		**IN ADDITION**	
Casket	1,250.00	Casket	1,250.00	Casket	1,250.00
Average cost of a casket of cloth or wood within a range from $500.00 to $3,000.00				Average cost in a nonprofit cemetery of a single grave, carefund, opening/closing charges, and grave liner, as per Final Disposition Chart.	
PLUS		**PLUS**		**PLUS**	
Cremation (315.00)		Cremation (305.00)		Cremation (363.00)	
OR		OR		OR	
Cemetery charges	1,500.00	Cemetery charges	1,500.00	Cemetery charges	1,500.00
(See Final Disposition Chart)		(See Final Disposition Chart)		(See Final Disposition Chart)	
Total	4,250.00	Total	3,795.00	Total	4,789.00

SAMPLE 2 — Continued
FINAL DISPOSITION: Step 3
(Local Cost Comparison — Chart 4)

CEMETERY COSTS

	Grave	Care Fund	Opening/Closing	Grave Liner	Total
Nonprofit	$ 600.00	$ 150.00	$ 450.00	$ 300.00	$ 1,500.00
Profit	$ 650.00	$ 162.50	$ 420.00	$ 540.00	$ 1,772.50
Religious	$ 500.00	included	$ 500.00	not required	$ 1,000.00

CREMATION COSTS

	Cremation Fees	Cremation Container	Urns
Funeral Home A	$ 285.00	$ 30.00 / 145.00	$ 125.00 / & up *
Memorial Society	$ 305.00		
Funeral Home B	$ 295.00	$ 68.00 / 203.00	$ 276.00 / and up *

* May not be of comparable construction, material, or quality

There is hardly anything made by man that cannot be made cheaper and sell for less.

Professional-Service Fees

One of the major concerns in any discussion of costs and planning is the professional-service fee. When I started in the funeral business, the price of a funeral was entirely dictated by the casket. Overhead and all other costs were factored in to the price of the casket. Back then, all funerals then called for a casket and it was a simple way to show all-inclusive costs. The major problem was that if the majority of the people in a community chose medium-price rather than expensive caskets, the funeral home would be unable to recover its overhead costs.

To deal with this problem, the funeral industry tried a new approach. It charged a basic fee for most of its services encountered in the immediate disposition portion of the funeral process. This guarantees an equal return on investment and overhead costs prior to choosing a casket.

One of the major differences between funerals organized by a memorial society and those that are not is the professional-service fee. Investment and overhead costs are included in the packages of services that are negotiated by the society with the contract funeral director. Those packages include the investment and overhead costs.

When comparison shopping, you will find that some funeral homes list a professional fee and others do not. These fees vary considerably. I strongly suggest that you do three things:

1. Decide on details of the funeral you wish to purchase.
2. Approach any of the funeral directors with your plan.
3. Ask for a specific price taking into account all items and charges, including the professional service fee.

Based on that final quote from each funeral home and your personal preferences for one establishment over another, you can make your final choice.

Merchandise

Funeral-home charges are broken into two categories. The first relates to the services that are provided by the staff and the overhead costs, including the use of facilities. The second cost relates to the actual merchandise that is offered by the funeral home.

Caskets

This is usually the most costly item of merchandise. Caskets are primarily designed to show a body. Some caskets have full openings, but these are rare. Most caskets have a half-opening that allows the body to be seen from the waist up.

Today, the casket is still the most popular way to hold and display a body, but two other options are now available. The first is a burial container. With more and more people choosing not to be viewed, the need for the traditional display casket is decreasing. The second option is for those that choose direct disposition with no service. In the case of cremation, a wooden, cardboard, or plywood container may be used.

In my community, this means that a display casket can be purchased for less than $500 or for as much as $5,000. If a container is chosen, it can be purchased from as low as $30 or as high as $1,000.

Rental is also an option. If you wish to use a display casket but are reluctant to have it buried or burned, you may rent a casket for viewing and/or a commemorative service. For final disposition the body is encased in a container. This option can halve your cost for the full use of a casket.

Caskets usually come in three different types:

- *Cloth covered:* various colors and textures
- *Hardwood:* a full range of woods including mahogany, oak, ash, and poplar
- *Metal:* various metals, including copper or steel, with a variety of finishes

Metal caskets are also available in the higher price range and include a monoseal to protect the interior of the casket from water.

Urns

In cremation the ashes are often placed in an urn. The urn, like the casket, is simply a container to hold human remains. The ashes may then be scattered from the urn, buried, or placed in the niche of a columbarium.

Urns are sold in various forms and at various prices. They can be made of plastic (for shipping), hardwood, marble, metal, or porcelain. Some urns are designed to hold the remains of two people, such as a couple. The price range in my locality is as low as $30 for plastic urns to more than $2,000 for metal urns with artwork.

Vaults

In many cemeteries, grave liners or burial rough boxes or vaults are required for the burial of cremated remains. The material used can vary from wood to concrete to metal such as stainless steel, copper, or bronze. Costs vary, as with caskets and urns, from a few hundred dollars to more than $3,000.

Memorial markers or monuments

In the past, stone works specializing in cemetery memorials usually sold monuments and statuary. As more cemeteries demanded flat markers to improve maintenance procedures, memorial markers became popular. Most funeral homes sell these markers. They may be of stone, usually granite or metal.

The six ways to
pay for a funeral:

1. Cash

2. Check

3. Credit card

4. Assignment of
Life Insurance
proceeds

5. Approved bank
financing

6. Proceeds from a
prepaid funeral
plan

Prices vary and, depending on the composition and size, they are usually priced from $500 to more than $1,500. The cost of larger traditional monuments, where allowed, varies accordingly.

Payment and Prepayment

Fifty years ago, when I first entered the industry, the account was submitted to the deceased's estate. Some funerals were paid for by agencies or government services, and some were paid for in cash immediately or shortly after the funeral from the proceeds of an insurance policy.

All of those options remain today, but two other options, not available in my time of service, have been added:

• Credit card

• Funeral financing

Credit cards with limits in the $10,000 range allow for a full range of services and merchandise. For people who use credit cards to earn points, this is simply one more purchase that allows for that option. It may seem a bit unusual to earn Air Miles with your funeral purchase, but today's consumer has not only purchase options but also can take advantage of all other types of options.

In one brochure I obtained from a local funeral director, there is a list of 18 various plans, policies, organizations, and societies that offer payment options for a funeral. The options differ greatly but this illustrates that funeral financing is a reality in today's market.

Planning in advance of death allows you time to evaluate these different options and choose the one that is right for you. When you speak to your local funeral directors, include payment and prepayment in your list of questions.

Death benefits

People are not always aware of death benefits when choosing a funeral. In certain cases, there are federal, state, or provincial programs that carry specific death benefits. Your funeral director will have experience and knowledge of the various benefits. He or she will not be able to determine your eligibility, but they will be able to give you the contact information. This information may impact considerably on the decisions you make concerning the goods and services that you choose.

8
QUESTIONS AND ANSWERS

There is a great deal of information in this book, and for some who are looking at it for the first time, it may seem like a lot of reading. This chapter is dedicated to giving quick but informative answers to many of the most commonly asked questions.

Funerals

Why do we have funerals?

Funerals are the customary way to deal with death in our society. They have been held in one form or another since 35,000 BC. It is a ritual for the living to help them deal with their grief and to honor the memory of the deceased.

How big is the funeral industry?

In the United States, the following figures will give you an idea of the size of the industry:

- There are more than 22,000 funeral homes.

- There are more than 115,000 cemeteries.

- There are approximately 1,115 crematories.

- The nation's funeral homes and cemeteries represent a reported 20-billion-dollar industry, performing slightly more than two million funerals a year.

- It is estimated that more than 50 billion dollars is being held in escrow for those people who have prearranged their funerals.

What does a funeral director do?

The funeral director is the principal advisor and primary resource person for those arranging the funeral. Funeral directors are professional caregivers and administrators who act with and for the family in all aspects pertaining to death. This can be done either by direct service or by appropriate referrals for specific items, or by providing information based on their training and experience. They are the representatives of the funeral home and offer a wide range of options concerning funeral-related merchandise. Throughout the United States and Canada, state or provincial funeral authorities usually license funeral directors. The requirements include education, training, and fulfillment of professional experience standards.

Do I have to use a funeral director or funeral home to bury the dead?

The laws vary from jurisdiction to jurisdiction. Some places, such as New York, require the services of a funeral director to handle the legal requirements. Other jurisdictions do not. Your local funeral directors can answer this question.

According to law does a body have to be embalmed and what is the purpose of embalming?

There are no longer legal requirements to embalm but some transportation carriers are reluctant to accept remains for shipping that are not embalmed. Embalming retards decomposition, sanitizes, and enhances the appearance of the body for public or private viewing. Restorative practices and cosmetics also allow the body to be shown if it has been disfigured by a traumatic death or illness.

Why should the public view a body?

The viewing of a body after death, in a casket prior to burial is a cultural tradition in North America. Some grief counselors believe that viewing is helpful in the grief process and in the acceptance of the reality and finality of death. The practice, however, is decreasing. The trend today, in many parts of North America, is towards either a closed casket or no body present at the memorial service. For some, this is a philosophical choice; for others, it is done to lower the overall cost of the funeral.

Cost

What does a funeral cost?

Funeral costs vary from less than $1,000 to more than $15,000. There are many factors in determining the cost of a funeral. The most important one is the type of funeral you decide to purchase. The cost depends on the options you choose in addition to the base costs. Your location, whether in a large urban center or small rural community, will also affect the cost. The following are reported average costs in various locations. Canadian locations are quoted in Canadian dollars, and the American in US dollars. You will note that there can be a considerable difference in prices. For a full discussion of prices, refer to Chapter 7. These following figures are taken from various reports, articles, and the Internet.

- The average cost of a funeral in the United States, as reported by the Funeral Directors Association of America, for 2001 was $5,108. This figure does not include the related cost of final disposition (burial or cremation charges and monuments or grave markers).

- The New York Funeral Directors Association in the year 2000 reported that the average funeral cost $4,580. This figure also does not include final disposition costs.

- The American Association of Retired Persons estimated the average cost of a funeral, including burial and monument, was $7,520.

- In Canada there are various estimates; however, one funeral home reports that the Ontario Board of Funeral Services statistics put the average cost at CDN $5,500. They also report that the average cost for a traditional funeral might be as high as CDN $7,500 (plus final disposition costs).

In my cost comparisons within my own area, I found a very wide price range. Immediate disposition of a body, without remembrance services but including cremation costs, could be obtained for less than CDN $800. A traditional funeral including casket, burial, and a monument could be priced as high as CDN $8,000. Most funeral homes in Canada and the United States must supply, on request, a price list for all the goods and services that they offer.

Options

How are funeral practices changing?

There have been a number of trends and permanent changes in the past 30 or 40 years. Some of these occurred because of the changes in the public's perception and attitude toward death. Other changes have been driven by the funeral industry itself. These changes include —

- increase in use of cremation for final disposition;
- decrease in religiously based services or clerically conducted funerals;
- a growing number of remembrance services held without a body present and focused on the celebration of the life of the deceased;
- fewer open caskets for viewing of the deceased;
- fewer flowers and increased use of donations to charities as an expression of sympathy;
- a trend towards dignified simplicity and lower-cost funerals;
- more prearranged and prepaid funerals;

- more immediate disposition (no remembrance service) type of funerals; and
- a change of the funeral-home ownership pattern from sole proprietor, one-location establishments to chains of corporate funeral homes.

Do I have to buy a casket?

No. Traditionally, a casket has been used to encase the body for burial or cremation. It was also part of the focus of the viewing and visitation tradition. Today, you may choose not to use a casket if you wish to have a memorial service during which the body is not present.

You may also rent a casket. Whether or not you use a casket, you must purchase some kind of container for either burial or cremation. These containers are usually much lower in cost.

Is it legal to scatter ashes?

Yes. Throughout most of the United States and Canada, it is legal and allowed. They may be scattered on public land or private land with the owner's permission. They may also be scattered on water. There are a number of considerations:

- Is it a location that you or your family might be able to visit in the future?
- Does it have meaning within the life of the deceased or the family?
- Who should do the scattering and when?

Ashes may also be buried in a single or family plot you already own. Check with the cemetery to see that it is allowed and find out the cost. Most cemeteries have a special location for the burial of ashes, or you may be able to place them in a niche of a columbarium that is designed to hold ashes and usually displays a memorial marker or plaque.

What is embalming?

Embalming is a procedure of fluid injection into a body to sanitize and delay decomposition. It is not required except in some instances in which a body is being shipped by a common carrier.

What is cremation?

It is a method of final disposition. The body is placed in a specially constructed furnace called a retort chamber. The chamber is heated to approximately 2000 degrees Fahrenheit for several hours. This process reduces the body to an approximate weight of between four and nine pounds of ashes and bone fragments.

9
COMPLETING YOUR FINAL FUNERAL PLAN

Now that you have —

- read and understood all your options in the three phases and process of planning a funeral, and
- compared local costs and services available to you,

it is time to make your choices by completing a statement for each of the three phases.

Be prepared to answer the following questions:

Statement 1: Immediate Disposition

If you don't want a funeral service —

- have you decided which funeral home or memorial society will be contacted at the time of death?
- have you decided to have no funeral commemorative service but want a direct burial or cremation?
- have you decided between burial or cremation? (See Statement 3 for final-disposition instructions.)

Statement 2: Remembrance Services

If you want a commemorative or memorial service to be held —

- have you decided which funeral home or memorial society will be contacted at the time death?
- have you decided on burial or cremation? (See Statement 3 for final-disposition instructions.)

- have you decided to have a commemorative service (body present) or a memorial service (no body present)?

- do you wish to be embalmed, have a casket, and be viewed by the public, family only, or have a closed casket?

- have you decided on a religious service or a secular service, and if you chose a religious service, will it be in a church or funeral chapel?

- have you decided on clergy, music, suggestions for pallbearers, etc.?

- if you choose a secular service, where will it be held?

- who will conduct the service and who would you like to participate?

- do you wish your military of fraternal affiliations to be part of the service?

- have you decided on the type and cost of a casket, if one is to be used?

- have you decided about flowers or, in lieu of flowers, that donations be made to a charity, and if so, which one?

Statement 3: Final Disposition (Burial or cremation)

If you have chosen burial —

- do you wish a single grave or do you want to purchase a number of graves to form a family plot?

- have you decided on the location of the cemetery and will you purchase now or at the time of death?

- have you decided whether you want a grave liner or vault, and if so, what type and within what cost range?

- have you decided if you want a monument, and if so, what type and within what cost range? Do you want any special wording?

- do you wish to have a public or private committal (burial)?

If you have chosen cremation —

- have you chosen the crematory and the type of container to be used?

- have you decided whether you wish your ashes to be buried, placed in a columbarium, or scattered? and if scattered, by whom and where?

If you can now answer yes to all the above questions, you are ready to complete your funeral plan. You will note that there can be as many as 20 important choices to be made in the normal process of a funeral. Once again, remind yourself that if you do not plan now, all these decisions will have to be made by your loved ones at a time of great emotional stress. By completing the appropriate statements now, you will have saved them from making those decisions, and you should have saved a considerable amount of money as well.

If you have decided on immediate or direct disposition, please complete Statements 1 and 3 (Appendixes C and E).

If you wish a commemorative service to be held, please complete Statements 1, 2, and 3 (Appendixes C, D, and E).

These statements form your completed funeral plan.

The final step is to place the statements with your personal information and any other special instructions you have, with or without a copy of your will, in a safe but accessible place (not a safety deposit box). Inform those who will be involved with your funeral arrangements that you have completed a funeral plan, and if necessary, discuss it with them.

As the years pass, you may wish to adjust or alter the decisions that you have made at this time. That can be easily done. These are not legally binding documents.

10
OTHER INFORMATION

This book is designed to provide basic information for residents of the United States and Canada. The basic information is relevant and common to all areas within that jurisdiction, but geography can influence attitudes, philosophies, and practices concerning death and disposition.

The most striking example of that can be found in the statistics concerning cremation. In the United States, 13 of the 15 most western states have cremation rates of 35 percent to 70 percent. In the south, 10 of the 15 states have the lowest rates: 7 percent to 15 percent. In Canada, in Newfoundland and Labrador, only 13 percent of final dispositions are done by cremation. On the west coast of Canada, in British Columbia, the figure is 75 percent, the highest in all North America.

Different philosophies and attitudes about death are clear in even that one option. In revisiting my profession and researching this book, I was pleased to note that the Internet now provides a wealth of information about every aspect and on every topic dealing with death and funerals.

While this book is designed to condense and simplify the available information, I refer you to the Internet as an incredible resource on all aspects of death and dying. I have listed various links that I found useful and informative.

International and national associations provide membership lists by state, province, and even local locations. They provide excellent information in all areas concerning death and funerals. Even individual funeral homes in specific cities offer local information. It would be cumbersome and unnecessary to list too many but I offer the following sites as excellent examples of the industry's attempts to educate the public, maintain professional standards, and present their particular views. Once again, education and information offer you options so that you may make well-informed choices.

Suggested Internet Links

National Funeral Directors Association (US)	www.nfda.org
Funeral Service Association of Canada	www.fsac.ca
International Cemetery and Funeral Association	www.icfa.org
Cremation Association of North America (INT)	www.cremationassociation.org
Funeral Consumers Alliance (US)	www.funerals.org
American Casket Retailers Association (US)	www.acra.org
National Casket Retailers Association (INT)	www.casketstores.com
Funerals with Love	www.funeralswithlove.com
Aurora Casket Company	www.funeralplan.com
The Preplanning Network	www.preplannet.com

Suggested Reading

Last Wishes: A Funeral Planning Manual and Survivors Guide	by Malcolm James & Victoria Lynn (Mavami Inc.)
Death to Dust: What Happens to Dead Bodies?	by Kenneth V. Iserson (Galen Press Ltd.)
Profits of Death: An Insider Exposes the Death Care Industry	by Darryl J. Roberts (Five Star Publications)
On Death and Dying	by Elisabeth Kubler-Ross (Scribner)
The High Cost of Dying: A Guide to Funeral Planning	by Gregory W. Young (Prometheus Books)
Caring for the Dead: Your Final Act of Love	by Lisa Carlson (Upper Access Book Publishers)
Purified by Fire: A History of Cremation in America	by Stephen R. Prothero (University of California Press)

APPENDIXES

This section is designed to provide you with forms and other material to help you complete your final funeral plan. It includes appendixes:

    A. Information Required for Registration of Death

    B. Contact List for Next of Kin

    C. Funeral Statement 1: Immediate Disposition Instructions

    D. Funeral Statement 2: Commemorative Services Instructions

    E. Funeral Statement 3: Final Disposition (Burial or Cremation) Instructions

APPENDIX A
INFORMATION REQUIRED FOR REGISTRATION OF DEATH

Full Name: _____

Address: _____

City: _____ State/Province: _____ Zip/Postal Code: _____

Home Phone Number: _____

Birth Date (month, day, year): _____

Birthplace (city, state/province): _____

Social Security/Social Insurance Number: _____

Marital Status (single, married, widowed, divorced): _____

Spouse's Full Name: _____

Social Security/Social Insurance Number: _____

Spouse Birth Date (month, day, year): _____

Marriage Date and Location: _____

_____

_____

Father's Full Name: _____

Father's Birth Date (month, day, year): _____

Mother's Full Name: _____

Mother's Birth Date (month, day, year): _____

Extended Family

Children (list oldest to youngest, include spouses and resident city):

_____

_____

_____

_____

_____

Number of Grandchildren & Names:

_____

_____

_____

Number of Great Grandchildren & Names:

_____

_____

_____

Number of Great-Great-Grandchildren & Names:

_____

_____

_____

Brothers/sisters (list oldest to youngest, include spouses and resident city):

_____

_____

_____

_____

Other Contacts

Family Physician: _____

Physician's Address: _____

Physician's Phone Number: _____

Next of Kin or Executor: _____

Relationship to Deceased: _____

Address: _____ Phone Number: _____

Additional Instructions: _____

_____

_____

_____

_____

Work History

Current or Last Occupation: _____

_____

Current or Last Employer: _____

_____

Years Employed: _____ Date of Retirement: _____

_____

_____

Military Service

Branch of Service: _____ War: _____

Discharge Papers Filed at: _____

Rank: _____ Served or Stationed at: _____

Eligible for Veteran's Disability (yes or no): _____

_____

_____

Religious Affiliation/Memberships

Religious Affiliations: _____

Church Groups/Membership: _____

Clubs/Lodge Memberships: _____

Professional Organizations: _____

Unions or Civic Group: _____

Other: _____

_____

Funeral Information

Contact Person:_____

Address:_____ Phone:_____

Type of Service Selected:_____

Contemporary Service:_____

Place of Service (funeral home, church, name of church):_____

Memorial Service (funeral home/church):_____

No Service:_____

_____

Type of Disposition (burial, entombment, cremation, or body donation):

_____

Name & Location of Cemetery/Mausoleum:_____

_____

Description of Lot or Mausoleum:_____

_____

Additional information required (newspaper obituary placement, music, and special readings):_____

_____

_____

APPENDIX B
CONTACT LIST FOR NEXT OF KIN

In the event of a death, the first notice is usually found in the obituary section of the newspaper or by word of mouth among friends and relatives. Often there are important people who should know as soon as possible, preferably from a member of the family. One member of the family or a close friend should be designated to contact the following people as soon as possible.

Immediate Contacts at Time of Death

Name:_____Telephone Number: _____ E-Mail:_____

Executor:_____

_____

Employer: _____

_____

Close relatives: _____

_____

_____

Friends:_____

_____

_____

_____

_____

_____

_____

_____

_____

Within Seven Days

Attorney:_____

_____

_____

_____

Life Insurance Agents:_____

_____

_____

Other:_____

_____

_____

APPENDIX C
FUNERAL PLAN STATEMENT 1: IMMEDIATE DISPOSITION

Upon my death, I wish to choose the option of immediate and final disposition without a memorial or commemorative service. I therefore instruct my executor or next of kin to proceed with that option.

After investigation of my local options available from my funeral providers, I wish

_____

(name of funeral provider)

to be in charge of completing these instructions.

I understand that their services will include the following:

- Arrangement conference to complete all necessary documents
- Completing and securing all relevant certificates registrations and permits
- Basic sanitary preparation dressing and care of remains
- Use of facilities to safekeep the remains and meet with the family

I have chosen not to have either a traditional or nontraditional funeral, but instead wish to have a direct disposition of my remains, without a funeral service. Please see Statement 3 for my final disposition wishes.

(Choose either burial or cremation.)

❏ I choose to be buried. I authorize the following:
- Removal of my remains from funeral home to cemetery
- Payment of cemetery fees, including purchase of grave(s) and opening/closing charges
- Grave liner or vault if desired or required _____
- Monument or marker if desired _____
- Completion of certificate of death

❏ I choose to be cremated. I authorize the following:
- Removal of my remains from place of death to funeral home and conveyance to crematory
- Payment of cremation fees
- Use of combustible cremation container.
- Completion of certificate of death
- Return of my ashes to my executor or next of kin

Check one of the statements below:

❏ I have prepaid the funeral provider for these services in the amount of $_____, with the understanding that this cost is fixed and locked in.

❏ I wish my executor or next of kin to pay the appropriate price for these services from my estate at the time of my death.

Signed: _____ Date:_____

APPENDIX D
FUNERAL PLAN STATEMENT 2: COMMEMORATIVE SERVICES OR CEREMONIES

Upon my death, I wish to have —

❑ a traditional service, with my remains present.

❑ a nontraditional service or celebration of life, with my remains
      (❑ body   or   ❑ ashes [check one]) present

        OR

❑ a nontraditional service or celebration of life, with my remains not present

The following are details of my preferences in the arrangement of my funeral service:

Traditional service

I wish to have a religious service conducted at my

❑ (church, synagogue, mosque),

_____ ,
(name of church, synagogue, mosque),

or at the

❑ chapel of the funeral home I have chosen.

If possible I would like _____ to conduct the service.
(Name)

My preferences in music, readings, or other details are as follows:

_____

_____

_____

_____

Nontraditional service (secular celebration of life)

I wish to have a service arranged by my family and friends in a location of their choice and with appropriate members of the family or friends participating in the service.

My preferences or suggestions for such a service are as follows:

_____

_____

_____

_____

In either type of service —

❑ Floral tributes will be accepted and appreciated, **OR**

❑ I would prefer that donations be made in my memory to:

_____

_____

In the matter of pallbearers (if appropriate), I would like my family to consider, if available:

_____

_____

In the matter of music, my preferences would be:

_____

_____

Signed: _____ Date: _____

APPENDIX E
FUNERAL PLAN STATEMENT 3: FINAL DISPOSITION

Upon the completion of any memorial or commemorative services, as outlined in Statement 2, I wish my remains to be:

_____

(cremated or buried)

If I am to be buried, my place of burial is to be:

_____

_____

(cemetery, grave, and plot location)

If I am to be cremated, I wish the final disposition of my remains to be:

❑ placed in an urn I have chosen or my executor or next of kin may choose:

❑ not placed in an urn

❑ buried (location and details):_____

_____

❑ placed in a columbarium (location and details): _____

_____

❑ scattered (where, how, and by whom): _____

_____

_____

_____

Check one of the statements below:

❏ I have prepaid $_____ for my burial or cremation with the understanding that the cost is fixed and locked in.

❏ I wish my executor or next of kin to pay the appropriate charges for these goods and services at the time of my death from my estate.

Signed:_____ Date: _____

TEAR-OUT WORKSHEETS

The following tear-out worksheets are for you to use when you enquire about the costs of the various good and services in your community.

They are duplicates of the charts used in the book to illustrate the costs that I found in my own community.

- **Worksheet 1: Memorial Society Options (by package)**

- **Worksheet 2: Immediate Disposition: Step 1**

- **Worksheet 3: Memorial Service: Step 2 (A)**

- **Worksheet 4: Traditional Service: Step 2 (B)**

- **Worksheet 5: Final Disposition: Step 3**

WORKSHEET 1

MEMORIAL SOCIETY OPTIONS

OPTION 1 IMMEDIATE DISPOSITION	OPTION 2 MEMORIAL SERVICE	OPTION 3 FUNERAL SERVICE
1. Transference of diseased to funeral home 2. Arrangement conference with next of kin/executor 3. Completion and filing of necessary documents, including registration of death 4. Minimum cost container for burial or cremation	* All items in Option 1, plus 1. Use of funeral-home chapel for religious or secular service 2. Staff for direction of service (without deceased present) 3. Transportation (one vehicle) for family, to and from service	** All items in Option 1, plus 1. Use of funeral-home chapel for religious or secular service (with deceased present — closed casket) 2. Staff attendance to direct service in church or funeral home 3. One vehicle to transport family to and from funeral and cemetery, and return
$ + recording fee	$ + recording fee	$ + recording fee
	Note: If family arranges the memorial service at their own location (church) and funeral-home staff are not required, only the charge for Option 1 applies.	**Note:** If pallbearers are used, the funeral home will supply one vehicle for transportation to and from location of service, to and from cemetery.
Not included	As in Option 1	As in Option 1
1. Goods and services tax 2. Cost of death certificates 3. Basic urn, cemetery costs, clergy honorariums, musicians, flowers, obituaries, embalming 4. Cremation fees 5. Transportation costs outside of 45 km (30 miles)		

WORKSHEET 2

IMMEDIATE DISPOSITION: Step 1

FUNERAL HOME A		MEMORIAL SOCIETY		FUNERAL HOME B	
Removal		Removal		Removal	
Facility use		Facility use		Facility use	
Arrangement conference		Arrangement conference		Arrangement conference	
Documentation & registration		Documentation & registration		Documentation & registration	
Body preparation		Body preparation		Body preparation	
		Membership & recording fee			
Cremation cost		Cremation cost		Cremation cost	
Container		Container		Container	
Total		Total		Total	

WORKSHEET 3

MEMORIAL SERVICE: Step 2 (A)
(No body or casket present)

FUNERAL HOME A		MEMORIAL SOCIETY		FUNERAL HOME B	
Removal		Removal		Removal	
Facility use		Facility use		Facility use	
Arrangement conference		Arrangement conference		Arrangement conference	
Documentation & registration		Documentation & registration		Documentation & registration	
Body preparation		Body preparation		Body preparation	
Use of funeral chapel		Use of funeral chapel		Use of funeral chapel or visitation room	
Staff for direction of services		Staff for direction of services		Staff for direction of services	
		Membership & recording fee		Professional service fee	
PLUS		PLUS		PLUS	
Cremation		Cremation		Cremation	
OR		OR		OR	
Cemetery charges		Cemetery charges		Cemetery charges	
(See Final Disposition Chart)		(See Final Disposition Chart)		(See Final Disposition Chart)	
Grand total		Grand total		Grand total	

WORKSHEET 4
TRADITIONAL SERVICE: Step 2 (B)

FUNERAL HOME A		MEMORIAL SOCIETY		FUNERAL HOME B	
Removal		Removal		Removal	
Facility use		Facility use		Facility use	
Arrangement conference		Arrangement conference		Arrangement conference	
Documentation & reg.		Documentation & reg.		Documentation & reg.	
Body preparation		Body preparation		Body preparation	
Use of funeral chapel		Use of funeral chapel		Use of funeral chapel	
Staff direction of services		Staff direction of services		Staff direction of services	
Vehicles (3)		Vehicles (1)		Vehicles (3)	
				Professional fee	
IN ADDITION		**IN ADDITION**		**IN ADDITION**	
Casket		Casket		Casket	
PLUS		**PLUS**		**PLUS**	
Cremation		Cremation		Cremation	
OR		OR		OR	
Cemetery charges		Cemetery charges		Cemetery charges	
(See Final Disposition Chart)		(See Final Disposition Chart)		(See Final Disposition Chart)	
Total		**Total**		**Total**	

WORKSHEET 5
FINAL DISPOSITION: Step 3

CEMETERY COSTS

	Grave	Care Fund	Opening/Closing	Grave Liner	Total
Nonprofit	$	$	$	$	$
Profit	$	$	$	$	$
Religious	$	$	$	$	$

CREMATION COSTS

	Cremation Fees	Cremation Container	Urns
Funeral Home A	$	$ / $	$ / & up *
Memorial Society	$		
Funeral Home B	$	$ / $	$ / and up *

* May not be of comparable construction, material, or quality

GLOSSARY OF TERMS

Casket or coffin: A box or chest for displaying and burying human remains. In North America, a casket's shape is rectangular, but in many other parts of the world it is hexagonal (six-sided) and shaped like a body. Our culture traditionally shows only the upper portion of the body. This container may be made of various materials, such as cloth-covered wood or composites, polished hardwood, or metals. A casket usually has handles to allow pallbearers to carry it.

Cemetery property: A single burial space is called a grave. More than one grave is called a plot. There may be two, three, or any number of graves in a plot, and if that plot contains all members of one family, it is referred to as a "family plot."

Cemetery services: This term refers to the graveside ceremony held immediately prior to burial. It may also refer to all the functions that are carried out by cemetery staff. These include the opening and closing of the grave, crypts, or niches; setting in place grave liners, burial vault markers; and long-term maintenance of the cemetery or the grave.

Columbarium: A structure with small spaces for the placement of cremated remains. The ashes must be stored in approved containers or urns. The columbarium can be outdoors or part of a mausoleum.

Cremation: The process of exposing human remains to intense heat to reduce the body to bone, which is then processed to a uniform size and consistency. The remains are referred to as ashes.

Crypt: A space in a mausoleum to contain either cremated or whole human remains

Disposition: The placement of the whole body or cremated remains in a final resting place. There are laws, regulations, and guidelines governing this act.

Entombment: Burial in a mausoleum

Grave liner: A wood or concrete inset for the grave to hold the casket

Interment: The burial of a body in the ground

Mausoleum: A structure in which human remains are entombed

Memorial service: A service commemorating the life of a deceased without the body present

Memorial society: A nonprofit organization that provides information and planned, low-cost funeral packages from a contracted funeral home

Obituary: A notice placed in a newspaper announcing a death and giving details of the deceased and funeral arrangements

Urn: A container to hold cremated human remains. Usually made of wood, metal, ceramics, etc. It may be placed in a columbarium, mausoleum, or buried in the ground.

Vault: An outer container to protect the casket, made of two separate parts and from material such as concrete, fiberglass, or steel. Some vaults have seals to keep out moisture.

Viewing/visitation: A time set aside at the funeral home when the family and public may pay their respects to the deceased